INSIDE AND OCCUPIED

INSIDE
AND
OCCUPIED

OVER 500 IDEAS FOR PARENTS WHOSE CHILDREN "HAVE NOTHING TO DO!"

NANCY S. WILLIAMSON

HERALD PRESS
Scottdale, Pennsylvania
Kitchener, Ontario
1982

Library of Congress Cataloging in Publication Data

Williamson, Nancy S., 1935-
    Inside and occupied.

    Includes index.
    1. Creative activities and seat work.   I. Title.
GV1203.W7515   372.5   82-3139
ISBN 0-8361-3304-8 (pbk.)   AACR2

Bible quotations are from *The New International Version,*
Copyright © 1978 by The New York International Bible Society. Used
by permission of Zondervan Publishing House.

INSIDE AND OCCUPIED
Copyright © 1982 by Herald Press, Scottdale, Pa. 15683
    Published simultaneously in Canada by Herald Press,
    Kitchener, Ont. N2G 4M5
Library of Congress Catalog Card Number: 82-3139
International Standard Book Number: 0-8361-3304-8
Printed in the United States of America
Designed by Tom Hershberger

82 83 84 85 86 87 88 12 11 10 9 8 7 6 5 4 3 2 1

TO LEONE ACKERLAND
whose encouragement and congeniality
helped me stay at the typewriter,
who contributed her skills
in the proofreading.

CONTENTS

FOREWORD

For every parent who has heard the complaint from a bored child, "There's nothing to do," Nancy Williamson's *Inside and Occupied* will be a cherished gift—much like a Christmas stocking brimming with treats to delight the child's heart. This book overflows with creative suggestions gathered from the author's years of experience in Christian education with young children. Knowing that "children's play is their work," as she expresses it, she has provided an abundant collage of play ideas which offers children a chance to discover new interests and develop potential talents. As a mother of three, I would have gratefully welcomed her book on those rainy mornings when my noncreative mind couldn't think beyond Lego and checkers!

Those who have appreciated the caring philosophy expressed in *Living More with Less* by Doris Janzen Longacre (Herald Press) will enjoy the innovative, practical ways in which Nancy Williamson converts everyday materials found in our homes into wonderful toys. Through her eyes and specific directions, two milk cartons become colorful blocks; hardware catalogs, old spigots, pipes, and fittings collected in a "prop box" help an aspiring plumber; a coat hanger becomes a harp. Hopefully, her imaginative way of finding a toy lurking behind America's throwaways will be contagious, helping us to find other treasures in unexpected places. With the high price of store-bought toys, most readers will find the book has paid for itself after trying just a few of her projects.

In addition to her suggestions on recyclables becoming toys, Williamson tells how to build "organizers" from common materials to help children learn a variety of skills. A six-pack carton covered with cheerful Con-Tact paper becomes a storage caddy for art supplies, a coat hanger is transformed into a book holder, or a detergent box turns into a file cabinet.

In an era when busy parents often do things *for* children rather than *with* them, many of the suggestions in *Inside and Occupied* lend themselves to activities which families can do together. Collecting rocks or shells together on a summer vacation extends into a winter activity as one helps a child organize and label the collection as the start of a new hobby. Such moments also lend themselves to natural discussions on the wonders of God's diverse creation, the author suggests. Writing "50 Things That Make You Feel Good" not only develops a child's writing skills but opens up delightful and whimsical conversations helping adults understand the uniqueness of each child.

But I also appreciate that the projects in the book help children to enjoy themselves and their times alone. If parents faithfully spend moments exploring with children the joyous possibilities of life through art, music, drama, science, language, and physical activities, a child is likely to pursue these areas further alone. What a rich heritage to share!

Educators, church teachers, and parents who delight in children, but often feel "out of ideas," will appreciate the multitude of useful suggestions in *Inside and Occupied*. The only problem will be time to try them all—a welcome problem!

—Linda Hunt, Coauthor
Loaves and Fishes
The Love-Your-Neighbor
Cookbook for Kids Who Care

AUTHOR'S PREFACE

A child has the inherent right to be enveloped in a loving family situation. The family needs to love, encourage, inspire, guide, and teach the child who is in its care. And what better way to learn of God's love than through the closeness and sharing in a family environment.

The ideas presented in this book were selected to provide help in carrying out the above goals. Hopefully *Inside and Occupied* will be a springboard for your own creativity in achieving success while dealing with the uniqueness of each individual child.

Scriptures and quotes are presented to cheer, lift, stimulate, and inspire you in the daily routine of nurturing beautiful, well-adjusted, creative, and enlightened offspring who love God, their family, and themselves.

Today's homes build tomorrow's world.

Nancy S. Williamson
Lyle, Minnesota

NOTE: Parental guidance may be required for some activities which involve cutting and cooking.

BOXES, BURLAP, AND BABY FOOD JARS

CHAPTER 1

Train a child in the way he should go, and when he is old he will not turn from it. —Proverbs 22:6

The earliest experiences of children take place in the home. There, in the little world of family life, they begin to adjust to people and change, establishing habits of thought and action which develop character. As they absorb the love of parents, observe the care expended upon them, and participate in domestic activity, a feeling of belonging emerges and the corresponding sense of security so necessary to one's well-being.

Wouldn't it be wonderful if all children learned that they are important, cared for, listened to, and loved as persons who can also extend themselves in loving ways? Certainly there would be less failure and fear and more personal growth, intimacy, and happiness. Growing, developing children must be involved in what is going on around them and in some way feel they can shape their own future.

Children need activities that provide opportunities for physical, mental, social, and spiritual growth. They learn by using the five senses God gave them. They need to participate directly in seeing, hearing, smelling, feeling, and tasting.

Toys and other creative materials and equipment provide opportunities for children to use

13

several of their senses to become aware of God's love and to develop Christian ways of behaving toward others.

Children learn best by doing and, to children, doing is playing. Their play is their work. Play is children's way of preparing for adulthood. And playthings are the tools with which they learn about their future. "Doing" is childhood's way of experimenting with the world. It is not important to them to produce a "thing" in the adult sense. They just need the opportunity to use their own unique drive to master and to create. Therefore, the child's environment should contain appropriate materials and equipment which will stimulate learning through a variety of experiences.

We can help stimulate and encourage imagination and creativity by placing before children objects such as an empty can, a discarded spool, a cardboard box, and asking them to think of different ways in which the item might now be used.

Although—like ants which throw off their wings in becoming workers—most grown people have discarded their imagination before entering on actual life, the little ones still have it; and if there are no flowers, they will quickly make them. If the surrounding atmosphere is warm and genial, wakeful life will be a ceaseless joy; invention will never be exhausted, and the materials of pastime will never be far to seek; a few corks will improvise a fishing fleet, and sticks and stones a palace.

Expensive store toys in many ways are inferior to simple "home" toys, such as milk cartons, egg cartons, empty cans and boxes, pots and pans. These things are part of the normal daily life of young children who find it natural to reach out and experiment. What they see their mother using they want to use, too. "In the everyday experiences of the child," said Jean Piaget, the Swiss psychologist, "lie the origins of curiosity." Therefore, it is our responsibility to provide basic materials for the

He who helps a child helps humanity with an immediateness which no other help given to human creatures in any other stage of human life can possibly give again.
—Phillips Brooks

14

child's experimentation and creativity.

The wonderful thing about this responsibility of ours is that it costs us practically nothing. Items we might otherwise throw away are learning treasures waiting to be discovered.

Listed below are some of the items you may want to begin saving for those times when your children either "have nothing to do," or need to express themselves through the use of manipulative materials.

foam meat trays
plastic scraps
wallpaper samples
aluminum foil
popsicle sticks
boxes—all kinds/sizes
fabric scraps
foam packing pieces
wood scraps
carpet squares/samples
sandpaper scraps
wire, nails, bolts, nuts,
    washers, screws
old clothes
foam rubber
used light bulbs
coat hangers
corrugated cardboard
cartons—egg, cottage cheese,
    milk, yogurt
shirt/hosiery cardboards
newspapers
paper bags
buttons
ribbon, yarn, string, thread
old cookie sheets
sequins
straws

seed catalogs
chicken wire
clay flower pots
crepe paper, tissue
brass paper fasteners
chenille wire
walnut shells
cardboard rolls
envelopes
rocks, pebbles
greeting cards
cans—no sharp edges
plastic bottles
old jewelry
L'eggs eggs
sponges
spools
paper—all kinds, colors
paper and foam cups
magazines
shoe boxes
old keys
corks
empty ball-type deodorant
    bottles
eggshells
blank slides or movie film
tinsel

paper doilies
cup hooks
cookie cutters
cotton balls
shoelaces
cotton swabs
macaroni, rice
soap scraps
wrapping paper
baby food jars
pop can pull tabs
clocks, locks, hinges
aerosol can lids
bottle caps
pegboard scraps
Sunday school or school take-
    home papers
wood curls
magnets, thermometers,
    magnifying glasses
seeds, beans
burlap, felt
pinecones
white sheets, pillowcases
beads
clothespins
cigar/school boxes
paper clips

rubber bands
sawdust
old cameras
clear plastic sheets
Con-Tact paper scraps

toothpicks
shells
feathers
sand
Styrofoam pieces

A few items you may want to purchase include:

crayons
tempera paints
scissors
paintbrushes

water colors
liquid starch
white glue, paste
cellophane tape

Advice to mothers: Unless you deliberately set aside a little time for relaxation, you will not be able to care for your family efficiently. Therefore, plan to relax a minimum of an hour and a half every fifteen years or so.

The following chapters will provide hints and ideas on how these various items can be used by you and your children. Just a few are included here in order to get your thoughts going on the infinite possibilities for learning and creating with materials that often are considered junk. Where are you expected to keep all these things? You don't need to keep large quantities on hand, and most of the items are quite small so not too much storage space will be required.

When we have done our very best, God will do the rest.

USE COFFEE cans with plastic tops for storage whenever you can. They're nearly indestructible, easy to label, and look great when decorated in bright colors with enamel paints, Con-Tact paper, or a collage made from magazine pictures. Be certain there are no sharp edges on the cans before children handle them.

USE STACKING plastic vegetable bins (available in the houseware center of most hardware and department stores) for storing small toys and craft materials. Use a separate bin for each kind of toy or article so pieces don't get mixed up or lost.

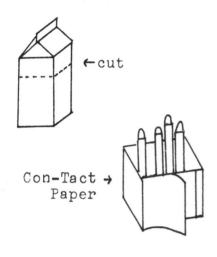

←cut

Con-Tact → Paper

MILK CARTONS also make sturdy containers for crayons, paintbrushes, chalk, pens, and pencils. They can be cut off to the appropriate size and decorated with Con-Tact paper or painted.

ADD A new dimension to the playtime by supplying inexpensive props. For playing hospital, make beds from small plastic foam meat trays. For patients, paint faces on clothespins or paste figures on popsicle sticks. Make them more authentic with a hospital gown. Fold a square of white material in half and cut gown shape with neck on fold. Clip hole in neck and put over head of "patient." Glue or staple the gown to hold it in place. Make a stretcher by stapling a piece of white felt between two popsicle sticks. Carry patients to the hospital in a shoe box ambulance. Cut a door in the end of the box; put a red cross on the side. Glue or staple a smaller box at one end for the driver's cab. Round cardboard wheels can be glued to the sides. Fill up at a gasoline pump. Using a tall, liquid detergent bottle, punch two holes about ¾ inch apart on the upper side. Pull heavy yarn through the holes and knot at one end. Tie a small spool on the other end for the gasoline spout. Put a piece of self-stick paper on the bottle and label it GAS.

Love, affection, ideas, and ideals should be gifts of parents to the home, and these are supplied by Christ.

SIMPLE FLOOR pillows can be made from old pillowcases and newspapers. Dye the pillowcases bright colors with household dye. Then starch and iron the dyed cases. Stuff them by neatly folding newspapers inside each pillowcase to make a mat. Snap fasteners or a strip of Velcro sewn to the edge of the pillowcase opening make it possible to remove the newspapers and launder the pillowcases. The newspapers can be changed as they wear out, but the pillowcases will last a long time.

BLOCKS can be made from 2 one-half gallon milk cartons. Open tops and wash thoroughly. Trim off ¼ inch flaps at top. Stuff one carton with wadded up newspaper, then insert it—open end down—into the open end of the other until one carton is inside the other. Cover with Con-Tact paper.

MAKE YOUR own geo-boards for a challenging and creative experience for your child. Carefully sand an 8 x 8 x 2 inch board so all rough surfaces are gone. With a ruler and pencil, mark the board into one-inch squares. Hammer a finishing nail at each one-inch interval. Let the child stretch rubber bands between the nails to make geometric designs.

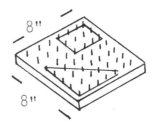

Doll Bed

Table

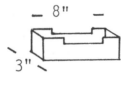

Range

USE HEAVY cardboard boxes to make "playing house" furniture. Cut the boxes as suggested in the sketches. Paint each piece with water-base paint. Draw details with a felt pen.

CREATE YOUR own games. Begin by collecting some large gift boxes—the collapsible, fold-flat kind. Found in your local department store, and probably in your local closet, these gift boxes can serve double duty in the making of games that require game boards.

First, the game board. Fold the box flat, cover with paper if necessary to achieve a plain surface, and draw the game board you have in mind. Cover the completed board with self-adhesive clear plastic for longer wear.

When the game board is popped back into a box shape, it becomes storage for the game's playing pieces, cards, score pads, directions, etc. And with the game board on the outside instead of hidden away inside, children should have no trouble in recognizing the game they're after.

RECYCLE the white plastic foam trays from packaged meat into dot-to-dot type activities. In this game, instead of drawing lines between dots, holes are punched and children connect the holes with yarn.

Parents spend the first part of a child's life urging him to walk and talk, and the rest of his childhood making him sit down and keep quiet!

Collect trays of all sizes. Lightly trace a pattern on the tray using a pencil. You may want to draw something appropriate to a particular season or holiday. Next, punch holes about ½ inch apart along the outline. Use an ice pick or pen to make holes about the width of a pencil. Trim any excess from the back of the tray.

Attach a piece of yarn to the first hole. Label the holes with numbers or letters for the child to follow as he threads the yarn through them.

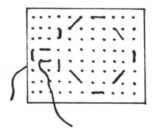

CUT A large sheet of pegboard into 9 x 12 inch pieces. Sand all edges smooth. If the pegboard is not prefinished, apply sealer to the smooth side and allow to dry. Then paint each board a pastel color, making sure paint does not fill the holes. After paint is thoroughly dry, sketch large simple outlines of flowers, trees, birds, apples, animals, numbers, letters, etc. on the boards. Outline each sketch with paint or felt pen of appropriate color. Give your child old shoelaces or yarn which had one end wrapped with cellophane tape or had been dipped in glue to make it stiff. He can then lace this through the holes following the outline.

You might also get some doweling to fit the holes in the pegboard and cut into 2-inch lengths to make pegs to use in place of the laces. Provide at least 25 pegs for each board.

THINGS always seem to break in a child's awkward world. To help them understand that things can be fixed or mended, let your children be a part of the fixing process. They can help glue or tape it back together.

OBTAIN scrap tubing, Plexiglas, and trimmings from plastics companies.

SAMPLE swatches and endpieces from rugs can be secured from carpeting stores.

CARDBOARD cores from bolts of material make great backings for bulletin boards. Check with your local fabric store to get some of these.

Nowadays you'll find almost everything in the average American home . . . except the family.

GARMENT factories are a great source for materials, yarn, buttons, scraps, and decorative notions.

BILLBOARD companies often have pieces of billboard to use for poster or other artwork.

ICE-CREAM stores are a source for 3-gallon ice-cream containers . . . great for storage.

ARCHITECTURAL firms, upholsterers, textile companies, cabinetmakers, wallpaper and paint stores provide color samples, tile samples, Formica squares, wallpaper books, and scraps of all kinds.

PAPER companies have paper delivered in large cardboard tubes which are usually discarded. These make good chairs, tables, cubbies, etc.

There are those who pray for eternal life who don't know what to do on a rainy afternoon.

JUNKYARDS and scrap metal yards offer unlimited possibilities! Wheels of all sizes, gears, moving parts from clocks, handles, knobs, hinges, and fittings.

BE ON the lookout for materials wherever you go. And when you find a good supply of an unusual material or item, ask for a bit more than you need to use at home and donate it to your local Sunday school, day-care center, or preschool.

A TRANSPARENT plastic tablecloth can be a useful item. Place pictures or patterns under the cloth and let your child draw on the plastic cloth. The crayon or felt pen can be rubbed or washed off and the cloth used again and again.

PEEP BOXES. You will need a shoe box, stand-up cutouts to illustrate a story, any necessary props to make the story complete, crayons, paste, cellophane, or Saran Wrap.

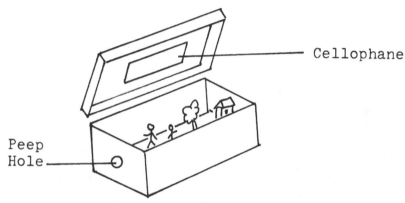

The shoe box may be painted with tempera paint if desired. Cut a large hole in the lid; cover the hole with cellophane or Saran Wrap. This lets light into the box. Cut a peephole in one end of the box. Arrange pictures and props inside the box to make a scene from a story. Use twigs stuck in clay for trees or shrubs, green toweling for grass. Put the lid on the box and peep through the end hole to view the scene.

CONSTRUCT "imagine" centers by turning large-sized cardboard boxes into switchboards, rocket ships, farm tractors, train engines, automobile dashboards, etc. By glueing on some spools, knobs, yarn, round cardboard discs, buttons, and drawing on speedometers, numbers and clocks, and cutting out windows where needed you will create quite an attention keeper. Place a chair or stool in front of the "imagine" box and your child will take over from there.

Don't expect a thousand-dollar answer to a ten-cent prayer.

21

GADGET BOARD. A gadget board will provide a type of activity that will help children learn manipulation, satisfy curiosity, and keep them out of cupboards. There are opportunities for teaching as you use the gadget board. The child can learn about locks, hinges, doorbells, keys, casters, etc. Attach these different gadgets onto a piece of plywood. Screw them down tightly. The child can manipulate the various parts of the locks, hinges, and keys while they are attached to the board.

Rejoice in the Lord always. I will say it again: Rejoice. Philippians 4:4.

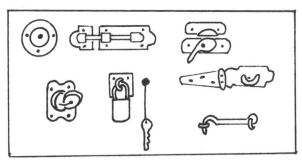

You can discuss safety while using this board. Explain why we have locks on doors and medicine cabinets. Discuss friendship when explaining how the doorbell works—how exciting it is when someone comes to visit and how happy we make others when we visit them.

When skill and love work together, expect a masterpiece.

MAKE MATCHING games from "L'eggs eggs" used to package women's hose. Draw different colored vertical and horizontal lines and other designs on the eggs with felt pens. Then, take the eggs apart, mix them up, and let your child sort them out and put the correct halves together. Upper and lower case letters could also be put on the different halves to be matched.

CONSTRUCT a miniature city from a large sheet of cardboard. Cut down a refrigerator packing box to get a sheet of cardboard about three feet square. With a crayon or felt pen, draw streets, rivers, and railroads. Use crayons or paints to make green grass, flowers, parks, blue water. The streets can be colored gray or black. Don't forget the yellow lines down the middle and the crosswalks at the intersections. Miniature trees, stop signs, street name signs, and buildings can be made from light-weight cardboard. Miniature people and animals can be made from clay, spools, or chenille wire. Now the city is ready to travel through. Cars, trucks, trains, and boats can make their way across town. This is a good toy to help teach traffic safety rules.

PLASTIC food storage containers of various shapes and sizes can be used to help children recognize basic shapes. They can be arranged according to size and shape.

NUTS, bolts, washers, and gears of all sizes help develop hand-eye coordination and reinforce fine motor skills. Your child can fit the nuts into the bolts, manipulate the gears, etc.

The electric razor took away the razor strop; furnaces took away the woodshed; tax worries took away the hair and the hairbrush. No wonder kids are running wild these days. Dad ran out of weapons!

PROP BOXES are "toys" that bridge the gap between play and real life. What interests is your child showing now? Does he or she talk about being a mechanic, astronaut, nurse? Prepare a prop box to stir the creative juices. This box will contain things that are used in a certain occupation. Obtain the child's help when preparing the box by asking what tools or implements would be needed for the particular occupation. What does a mechanic use when he repairs cars or bikes, trains, or planes? What does an astronaut need when he is about to visit the moon? Tools, flashlights, wires, proper clothing, etc.

The et ceteras are perhaps the most important things. These are what develop from the thoughts of your child and are what will keep the prop box from becoming stale. It will remain a never-ending learning tool. The props used in the boxes are real!

Real tools, real bandages, real binoculars, real curlers, and hairnets.

An example of a well-stocked prop box for an aspiring plumber would be: various lengths of pipe and fittings, spigots, plumbers wrenches, hose and nozzles, old shirt and cap, hardware catalogs, measuring tapes, etc.

A beautician's prop box might contain a mirror, curlers, hairpins, hairnets, old dryer, apron or large bib, combs, towels, magazines, empty plastic shampoo bottles, plastic basin, emory boards, and clear nail polish.

CUT OUT large magazine pictures of faces. Glue them on individual pieces of cardboard. Cut each face into three parts: just below the eyes, and just below the nose. Mix each group so they are not in their original order. Now punch a hole at the left side of each picture part. Place them in a three-ring binder. The picture parts can be turned to create different faces. This same procedure can be used with other types of pictures such as buildings, animals, flowers, foods.

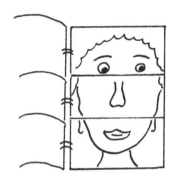

DO YOU have a budding architect in the family? If so, assemble a collection of boxes, wallpaper samples, carpet and cloth swatches, linoleum tiles, spools, Styrofoam pieces, corrugated cardboard, small plastic detergent bottles, etc. Cut away one side of each of several larger boxes to represent rooms. Stack the rooms to form a two-story house. Your child can determine which will be bedrooms, bathrooms, kitchen, living room, etc., and can then paper the walls, lay carpeting, and create furniture out of the other scraps. For example, chair shapes can be cut from a box side and mounted on spools. Different chairs can also be made by cutting two barrel shapes from detergent bottles and mounting them on bottle caps. Styrofoam cubes can be arranged into furniture.

Little Dorothy was biting herself on the arm when her day-care teacher cautioned that she might hurt herself. "Oh, I won't," Dorothy replied, "the dentist said I have soft teeth."

Some people drink at the fountain of knowledge, others just gargle.

MAKE YOUR own softballs by wrapping lengths of scrap material around and around and around. This was done in ancient biblical times to create balls, and is still a good idea for today. Cut the material into strips about one inch wide by two feet long. This is about the maximum length that is easy to work with, especially for a child working alone. Begin making the ball by folding the material into as tiny a piece as you can. When you get to the end of one strip of cloth just glue, tape, or sew the next strip to the end. Continue wrapping, going in different directions with each strip of material until you reach the desired size. The final end of cloth can also be glued, taped, or sewed to the ball to hold it together.

PLASTIC six-pack holders are great to hang mobiles from or cut into individual sections for use as picture frames.

"L'EGGS EGGS" form the body of many animals, such as a sit-up Easter bunny, turtle, or ladybug.

SMALL cereal boxes are the right size for making box animals when covered and decorated with construction paper.

EGG CARTONS can be used for counting games or as paint containers at the easel.

A MASON JAR makes an efficient greenhouse. Place jar on its side, add soil and plants, and water every two months.

COAT HANGERS can be shaped into circles and decorated with 2 x 6 inch strips of crepe paper for seasonal wreaths. Tie the strips all around the circle until it is full.

CRUSHED eggshells give a textured look in artwork; just glue them to your picture.

EMPTY SOUP CANS, covered with paper and decorated make nice pencil holders or other storage containers.

POPSICLE STICKS are useful as holders for small puppets, name sticks in seed planters, or for buildings and other constructions.

USE OLD nylon stockings to stuff animals. They're washable and soft.

DIFFERENT-SIZED empty paper tubes can be covered to create an interesting "Cylinder City." Stand them on end and glue them to a flat piece of cardboard. Draw on windows and doors. Make cone- or flat-shaped roofs for the cylinders.

BULLETIN BOARDS are great when made from large mattress, refrigerator, or TV packing boxes. They can be painted or covered with construction paper, burlap, or any other type of material and either fastened to the wall or leaned against it.

A father who wants his children to get an education these days may have to pull some wires: the TV, telephone, stereo, and ignition.

STACKING BOXES are made from small- and medium-sized boxes covered with Con-Tact paper, wallpaper, or wrapping paper. Attach colorful cutout alphabet letters, numbers, or pictures to the sides.

CUT ROUND or square target boards from heavy cardboard. Mark the center and young children can toss beanbags at them. For older children, turn them into math devices by dividing each target face into 10 spaces. Assign one number to a space, and your targets are ready to use for addition, subtraction, or multiplication games.

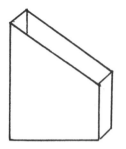

CLEAN large detergent boxes, cut off tops on a slant, and use for files. Cover entire box with Con-Tact paper. Your file is ready for magazines, children's record albums, paperback books, pamphlets, children's papers, etc.

HINGED furniture, cut and tape-hinged, can be built from large pieces of cardboard to become standing screens, space dividers, and bulletin boards.

A STUDY booth is a nifty item to make for your child. Select a cardboard box with a base about the size of a student's desk top. The base will be the floor, and one long side becomes the back wall of the learning booth. Slice diagonally down the two short sides of the box from the top of the back wall to the front edge of the floor. Then cut along the front edge and remove this portion from the box. Make sure the floor has an even writing surface. You might need to glue a flat piece of cardboard over it.

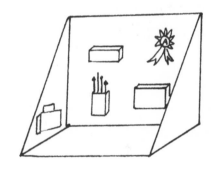

The booth is now ready for interior and exterior decoration. Cover it with paint or Con-Tact paper. Fasten small boxes on the interior walls to hold pencils, paper, etc. The booth is portable and is a good place for your child to do homework.

You might also want to make a booth that has a mirror on the back wall to use as a "grooming" booth. This can be used to help teach proper grooming habits.

MAKE a bookholder from a coat hanger. Hold the hanger so the hook is at the top. Squeeze the hanger arms together, bend the ends of the arms up and forward, and fold the hook down behind the arms. Colored tape wrapped around the wire makes the bookholder attractive as well as useful.

WASH OUT a coffee can. Then turn the can over and poke holes in the bottom with a can opener. Place one pair of scissors—points down—into each opening.

MAKE A stacking set of five or six food cans in graduated sizes that fit inside each other. Remove labels, wash cans thoroughly, and check to be sure there are no rough or sharp edges. Cover each can with Con-Tact paper, wallpaper, or wrapping paper. Cans can be stacked, lined up in order, or used for storage.

TO MAKE A CAR, remove the top and bottom from a cardboard box, approximately 11 x 17 inches long and 11 inches deep. With a pencil, sketch the outline of a car on the sides of the box. Paint the car with enamel paint. Add details with a felt pen. Your child steps into the carton car, holds it under his (or her) arms and "drives" it along as he walks. His feet and legs extend through the hole in the bottom of the box.

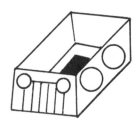

USE A 32-ounce, soft-drink six-pack carton covered with brightly colored Con-Tact paper as a sturdy storage caddy and carryall for games and art supplies. Then find six potato chip cans that will fit snugly into the compartments of the carton. Cover them with bright paper. Finish by labeling the lid of each can and fill 'em up!

A 24-compartment soft-drink crate makes a nifty portable mini-classifying center. Drop a tapered, flat-bottom paper cup into each compartment. Your child can sort nails, seeds, colored pieces of paper, buttons, etc., into the various compartments according to size, shape, or color.

IF YOU USE slide film when taking pictures and some of the slides come back blank or black, they can be recycled into original works of art. Use a cotton ball or tissue with household bleach and rub the slide to remove all the black color. Then your child can use felt pens or ball-point pens to draw on the slides. They can be viewed with your projector or through a battery-operated slide viewer. You can use the same process for movie film that did not develop correctly. Your child can "draw a movie."

Nothing lowers the level of conversation more than raising the voice.

SAVE OR COLLECT 300 bottle caps and turn them into a doormat about 16 x 20 inches in size. The best place to get caps is anywhere there is a soft-drink machine. Any kind of cap works, even the twist-off kind. Get a board the above size. Plywood works best, and should be at least ⅝ inch thick. Make rows with the caps (upside down) just touching each other. Drive a nail through the middle of each cap and into the board. The whole thing can be painted with spray paint. The mat is perfect for scraping the mud off dirty boots and shoes.

HERE ARE MORE things to save:

    graph paper
    newsprint
    wooden picnic spoons
    old gloves for puppets
    paraffin, old candles
    decals
    glitter

  Pictures: animals, children,
     holiday scenes, flowers,
     butterflies, insects, people,
     religious themes, tools,
     buildings, ships, planes,
     cars, trucks, foods,
     cartoons, sporting events, etc.

Kindness is one commodity of which you should spend more than you earn.

TRI-WALL CARDBOARD, the kind used for heavy-duty packing, can be used to construct many types of portable furniture. In fact, a tri-wall chair will easily support the weight of a heavy adult. You can use a bread knife or a handsaw to cut the cardboard. When planning how to cut the cardboard, be sure that the finished pattern will have the flutes (wavy sections) of the cardboard running up and down to give added strength. Additional strength can be achieved by adding a second layer of tri-wall and applying inexpensive white glue to the joints.

Keep smiling — it makes folks wonder what you're up to.

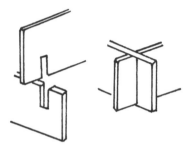

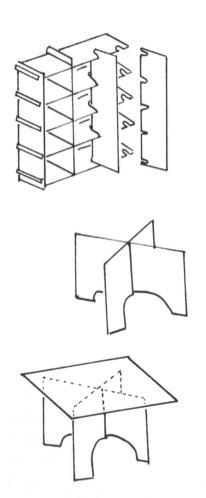

The strongest way of fitting sections together is by slotting and joining. For most constructions, each slot should be half as long as the piece into which it is being cut. Slots should be one-half inch wide, slightly narrower than the actual width of the tri-wall, to give a tight fit. Allow at least a 2½ inch overhang on the edge of an outside slot to maintain maximum strength in the cardboard. Tri-wall cardboard is available in single sheets or in quantity from many packaging-materials suppliers. Check your Yellow Pages under "packaging materials." Cost per sheet is about four or five dollars.

TREASURES AND COLLECTIBLES

CHAPTER 2

Do not store up for yourselves treasures on earth, where moth and rust destroy, and where thieves break in and steal. But store up for yourselves treasures in heaven, where moth and rust do not destroy, and where thieves do not break in and steal. For where your treasure is, there your heart will be also. —Matthew 6:19-21

Parents can help children build a healthy personality. Not the skin-deep kind you see on the billboards and in the movies. You can help your children build something deeper than that. You can influence how they feel; the kind of persons they are; the way they act; the kind of thoughts they have. You can help build their whole being.

You can help build the good feelings they will need, be they rich or poor, president or John Q. Citizen, doctor, lawyer, or merchant. You can help your children become happy and strong-feeling persons—persons who can see clearly their own problems but also the larger issues that affect every human being.

By providing a good playing environment we help our children develop into well-rounded persons. However, we sometimes get impatient when the play takes over the house. The mess and confusion and clutter get on our nerves and we have an urge to sweep it all out and tidy up. This urge can be particularly strong when youngsters collect things and then leave them scattered about. We say, "If they really cared about their horse pictures or baseball cards or racing cars or dolls. . . ."

31

What a man is depends largely on what he does when he has nothing to do.

But children do care. They may not seem to at times but these hobbies and collections and enthusiasms are their way of giving themselves something that the other fellow does not have. They are specialists. And in being specialists—knowing a little bit more, talking sometimes too much for what they know—they build themselves up. We all have a great stake in that.

With most of us, collecting is a habit that starts in childhood. Small boys and girls collect marbles or racing cars or miniature cups and saucers. Once you are hooked, you may be hooked for a lifetime. It is an absorbing game, a study in trial and error—you lose some and win some, but tomorrow is always another day, another adventure, and you can profit from your mistakes.

While hobbies are special interests which give pleasure in spare time, they also have a real value for a young person. Some hobbies such as history, science, or nature may lead to adult vocations. Others such as art, music, or stamp collecting may lead to lifetime enrichment. Hobbies provide a means of exploring God's great big wonderful world.

Here is a listing of some possible hobbies or special interest activities.

Collecting

books	leaves
buttons	Indian artifacts
paintings	stamps
poetry	postmarks
dolls	records, tapes
spider webs on paper	feathers
post cards	souvenirs
candles	bells
newspaper headlines	buckles
holiday traditions	jokes, riddles, tongue twisters

A good thing to
remember
And a better thing to do
To work with the
construction gang
And not with the
wrecking crew.

32

glassware
miniatures
insects
rocks
recipes
stuffed animals
antiques
photographs
cartoons
music boxes

coins
models (trains, cars, planes)
butterflies
holiday symbols
shells
dried flowers
doll house furniture
biographies
match books
most anything!

Much happiness is over-looked mainly because it doesn't cost anything.

Arts and Crafts

applique
block printing
pen-and-ink drawing
bread dough sculpture
sketching, drawing
embroidery
knitting
metalcraft
painting
pottery
sand painting
seed pictures
gift card making
rock sculpture
pom-pom figures
cardboard construction
mosaics
clay modeling
whittling
bead craft
costume design
dyeing
etching
leatherwork
rug making, braiding
basketmaking
calligraphy

poster making
ceramics
quilling
stained glass
quilting
totem pole construction
yarn hooking
chalk work
papier-mâché construction
toy making
woodworking, carpentry
candlemaking
crocheting
hat making
picture framing
banner making
mobile, stabile making
carving
crewel
decoupage
macrame
chenille wire sculpture
silk screening
sculpture
tin craft
dried vegetable jewelry
bookbinding

batik
design rubbings
driftwood sculpture
shell crafts
leaf printing
jewelry making
pattern making
paper curling
raffia
burlap weaving
peep boxes
paper dolls
wall hangings
apple dolls
weaving
tissue paper flowers
sand casting
petit point
felt crafts
plaster craft
3-D picture construction
stenciling
aluminum foil tooling
papermaking
touch and feel pictures
thumbprint pictures
corn husk dolls
silver smithing

Drama

charades
puppets
tableau
filmmaking
marionettes
pantomimes
readings
scenery making
play/script writing
storytelling
impersonations
mask making
play reading
stage craft

Music

instrument lessons
rhythm instrument making
composer research
picture collections of instruments/composers
tape making
voice lessons
record listening
music writing/composition
instrument research
sheet music collections
arranging
hymn illustrating
choral readings

He took a little child and had him stand among them. Taking him in his arms, he said to them, "Whoever welcomes one of these little children in my name welcomes me; and whoever welcomes me does not welcome me but the one who sent me."
—Mark 9:36-37

If you talk about your troubles,
And tell them o'er and o'er
The world will think you like them,
And proceed to give you more!

Mental Activities

book clubs
mental games
reading
creative writing
radio transmitting
pen pals
designing
family newspaper writing
diary/daily log writing
guessing games
puzzles
magic
research
historical study
missions study
memorization
paraphrasing
conversation/discussion

Nature/Science

indoor/outdoor gardening
animal research
weather study
flower arranging
rock hounding
pet care
tropical fish
astronomy
flower drying
insect research
leaf printing
space exploration study

mechanical building and drawing
medical/scientific research
inventing
rocks, shells, driftwood
electronics
radio construction
geology
geography
bird watching/study
mapmaking

U.S. history research	cooking
doll house decorating	gift making
knot tying	prehistoric research
occupations research	sewing
kite making	foreign language study
scrapbook keeping	origami
archaeology	sports research

TURN your children's collections into real learning projects. For instance, if they are collecting rocks, help them discover that rocks, with their endless variety and beauty, are a fascinating part of God's creation. Some activities connected with rock collecting include:

—Observing, telling what they discover by sight only. Rocks have different colors. They are all sizes and have different shapes.

—Handling (with eyes closed), telling what rocks feel like—bumpy, scratchy, smooth, sandy, etc.

—Classifying, grouping (1) heavy rocks and lightweight rocks, (2) smooth rocks and rough rocks, or (3) small rocks and large rocks.

—Exhibiting, glueing rocks to 3 × 5 inch cards, noting where the rock was found.

As your children participate in these activities, guide them to see the wonder and perfection of God's creation by asking questions such as, "What is especially beautiful (or interesting) about these rocks that God made?" Similar activities and questions can be used with shells, leaves, and other such items that children collect.

*Lord, who am I to teach
the way
To little children day by
day,
So prone myself to go
astray?
I teach them love for all
mankind
And all God's creatures,
but I find
My love comes lagging far
behind.
Lord, if their guide I still
must be,
Oh, let the little children
see
A teacher leaning hard on
thee.*
—*Leslie Pinckney Hill*

COLLECT some personalized facts. Check with your library to research old newspapers and magazines to learn what else happened on the date of your birth. What other important events took

This is the beginning of a new day. God has given me this day to use as I will. I can waste it or use it for good. What I do today is important because I am exchanging a day of my life for it. When tomorrow comes, this day will be gone forever, leaving in its place something that I have traded for it. I want it to be gain — not loss, good — not evil, success — not failure, so that I shall not regret the price I paid for it.

place that day? Who was the mayor of your town? Who was president of the United States? What was the weather like? What happened in the world of sports? What were prices like as compared to today? What other famous people share the same birthday as you? Obtain copies of newspaper headlines, magazine articles, and pictures of the various happenings on your birthday and keep a scrapbook. You can add to it each year as you keep a running record of "BIRTHDAY HAPPENINGS."

Start with the day of your birth and compose a timeline of your life. Chart the major events . . . first shots or immunizations . . . first day at preschool or kindergarten . . . first bicycle . . . first prize or award . . . first club meeting . . . baptism . . . received first Bible . . . attended first "big" party . . . first trip away from home overnight . . . etc. Pictures can be drawn on the timeline to illustrate the various events. Drawn on shelf paper, the timeline can roll up for storage. Or it can be hung around the top of the wall of your room with space for additions of future events. Goodness, what a history!

USE MILK cartons to make a showcase for your collections. Thoroughly wash and dry half-gallon milk cartons, one carton for each section you need for your showcase. Cut off the folded top of each carton. Staple the cartons together and cover the outside with colorful paper or paint. Make a label for the showcase, or label each section if desirable.

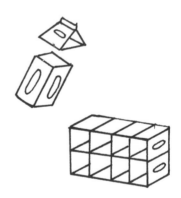

A SHADOW box type of display might be used for some collections. You will need a shallow box, like a hosiery box, and some paper to cover it. Attach a picture hanger to the back of the box to hang it on a wall.

AN OLD FISHNET can be used as a "bulletin board" to hang objects from. Suspend the net lengthwise from ceiling to floor in a corner. Or stretch it to cover an entire wall to create a large display area. Use paper clips for hangers. Unbend them to form an "S" shape. Attach one end to the display item and the other end to the net. One advantage of this type of display is that young children can put up and take down their own work without staples, pins, or tacks. And it makes a decorative display arrangement.

Character is determined not by single acts but by habitual conduct.

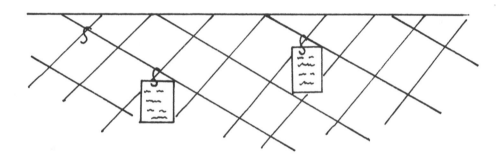

Life must be worth living—the cost has doubled and yet we still hang on.

HELP YOUR young child learn colors by starting a scrapbook of things that are all one color or a collection of objects that are all one color. For instance, a "blue collection" of buttons, yarn, paper, marbles, etc.

MAKE A game collection. Was a new game played in school or at a party? Write down the rules and instructions and compile them in a book of *Games I Like to Play*. The book can be divided into three sections: outdoor games, indoor games, games from foreign countries. These games can be shared with your friends. Inviting other boys and girls to join in your games is a good way to make new friends. The Bible says, "A man that hath friends must shew himself friendly" (Proverbs 18:24, KJV).

HERE'S AN activity that's made to order for all those children who "collect" interesting facts (about anything at all). Start collecting any facts that strike you as interesting; jot them down to be filed in scrapbooks. There can be books of "Funny Facts," "Historical Facts," "Religious Facts," "Weather Facts," etc. Some sample facts are:

1. What word describes a type of roofing material and is also a signboard outside a doctor's office? (a shingle)

2. Who is supposed to be the last person to abandon a sinking ship? (the captain)

3. In which of the 50 states does the dawn first greet the nation? (Maine)

4. What is the normal temperature for a human body? (98.6°F)

5. What are the two middle letters of our alphabet? (M, N)

I will praise you, O Lord, with all my heart; I will tell of all your wonders.
—Psalm 9:1

A 3-D CORNER is a fine way to display collections. Fold a large piece of cardboard to make it stand. Then fasten various small boxes (Kleenex, shoe, etc.) to the cardboard. They can be painted or covered with Con-Tact or wallpaper. Stand your collectibles on the tops of the boxes and you have a very interesting display.

PENS, PENCILS, PAPER, AND PERSONAL PROCLAMATIONS

CHAPTER 3

All your sons will be taught by the Lord, and great will be your children's peace.
—Isaiah 54:13

The child comes into the world endowed with infinite possibilities. These are but promises; they are still in embryonic form. The powers of mind and soul at first lie dormant, waiting for the awakening that comes through the touch of the world about and for the enlightenment that comes through instruction.

Let's face it—parents are a child's most important teachers. Not of facts, particularly, but of values. The growth of Christian personality is founded upon small beginnings that are made in early childhood. Thus, in these early years, it is important that children learn to do things for themselves, to play happily alone and with others, to use toys and other materials constructively, to begin to be willing to share their possessions, to treat friends and pets kindly.

If children are to grow to be wholesome individuals, they must know the joy of succeeding and of being commended for their successes. Failure should be met with understanding help so the young child will grow in the ability to live constructively.

Young children can grow to be thoughtful,

In the breast of a bulb
Is the promise of spring;
In the little blue egg
Is a bird that will sing;
In the soul of a seed
Is the hope of the sod;
In the heart of a child
Is the kingdom of God.
　　　—William L. Stidger

self-reliant, self-controlled individuals only insofar as they see these qualities at work in the lives of their parents and teachers. Through all of these early experiences, we can help little children to grow to be emotionally stable individuals, increasingly aware of God as a friend who loves and helps them every day.

Growth, however, does not come merely through giving of ourselves to children. It also comes through children giving of themselves. They need to balance intake with output, impression with expression. The child who expresses creativity through writing is exhilarated by the experience. However in creative writing, as in any creative activity, the main part of the experience lies in the degree to which it is the spontaneous outpouring of the child's imagination, experience, or idea. Although children create out of imagination, the well must be replenished with fresh experiences and literature which expose them to rhythm, rhyme, beauty, and sparkling, scintillating words. Without experience children have little to communicate. How can they write of things they have never seen?

Children differ in abilities in writing as they do in other creative activities. For some, the mere opportunity to write is enough. There is simply a sharing of ideas, feelings, and imaginings. Creative writing appeals to the senses and the emotions. It is a tremendous outlet for the inner self.

Children need an environment of psychological safety in which they are free to express their ideas. We can help by providing stimulating experiences; by allowing time to explore, experiment, and create; by supporting them during the creative activity; by supplying the needed tools; by helping make words come alive; by prompting them to become more aware, more perceptive, and more sensitive to people and phenomena; and by planning opportunities for them to share their writing with others.

We are not called upon to evaluate these writing experiments. Evaluation belongs with the child. The purpose of creative writing is artistic self-expression. Evaluation must be based on the extent to which children grow in the ability to express their ideas in a manner satisfactory to themselves at any given point in their development.

Not all children will find writing their favorite mode of creative expression. But every child can know to a degree the delight that begins with curiosity and ends in wonder. How satisfying to put into words the feelings of the afternoon in the first storm of summer, of watching a dark cloud come out of the west, cover the sun and send peals of thunder, shafts of lightning, and torrents of rain, where moments before birds were singing and clouds floated lazily across the sky as the child lay on the velvet green grass. Such a child in the final phase of creating finds the communicating of his idea to another the capstone of the experience.

There are many ways in which children can express themselves through creative writing. The following ideas suggest methods for experimentation with painting pictures with words. Some are appropriate for young children—some for older ones. You might even want to try some of them yourself!

Many families yearn for two things: First, to own a home; second, to own a car so they can get away from it.

KIDS AND stacks of paper often add up to clutter and waste. Use a plastic or wire LP record rack to vertically store small quantities of the different kinds of paper you have for use. The child will find it easier to get at the paper and you'll be better able to control usage and keep things in order.

When looking for faults, use a mirror, not a telescope.

PROVIDE a variety of pictures for your children to study. Have them choose one and write a brief story about what they think happened in the picture. You can help by making suggestions to stimulate imagination such as, "What do you think happened before the picture was taken?" or "Why are the people doing what they are?" or "How do the people in the picture feel?"

WRITING simple rhyming couplets can lead to original expressions of all sorts of truths and insights by children. A couplet is simply two short lines that have rhyming last words. For instance:
>God made the fish
>That go swish-swish.

Think of all the possibilities that are to be found in this method of creative expression!

PERHAPS your children have not yet begun to write. They can still share an experience with words! Get out a pencil and some paper and let them dictate their story to you. As they speak the words, you put them on paper. When finished, go over the story with them, pointing out the words as you read it together. Most likely they will be able to take that paper and "read" the story to other members of the family in future times of sharing. These stories can be bound together to make a book for them to keep. They can color a picture on construction paper for a book cover. Then punch holes along the left side of the pages and tie a piece of yarn through them.

What are children saying in trying to communicate with their parents?

Love me! I need you!
Respect me. I am an individual.
Trust me. I must learn to make my own decisions.
Accept me. And then let's be friends.
Be honest with me. Tell it like it is.
Listen to me. Maybe I have a good idea.
Forgive me. And then let's forget it.
Teach me of Christ — by your everyday life!
—Elizabeth C. Jackson

HOW ABOUT trying some "what-ifs?" Suggesting a thoughtful "What if . . ." question as the subject of a story places the child in a situation that may demand some deep rethinking of concepts.
"What if God had made the grass purple?"
"What if you lived in pioneer times?"
"What if you were a great doctor and discovered a cure for a terrible disease?"
"What if cats and dogs could talk?"

HERE'S AN IDEA that will not only motivate older children to creative expression, but will encourage Bible reading as well. Suggest some short chapters or verses for them to read. Then let them paraphrase what they have read. Paraphrasing is simply putting something into other words. If a child can paraphrase a Bible passage, it is a good clue that he or she really understands what the passage means. This learning experience helps children translate scriptural truths into the thoughts and experiences of today. It will cause children to look beyond the words to the real meaning behind them.

RECYCLE comic strips. Paste a piece of paper over the original words on a comic strip and write your own version of what is being said.

TRY "mirror writing" for an unusual project. The easiest way to do this is to put a sheet of carbon paper beneath a sheet of white paper—the carbon side toward the top sheet. Write on the top sheet. Then turn the sheet over and your writing will appear backwards. To read it, hold the paper in front of a mirror.

One doesn't find life worth living; he must make it that way.

WRITE a rebus story. A rebus story substitutes pictures for some of the words. Leave spaces where the nouns are supposed to be and draw pictures to represent them.

WRITE A mini-acrostic . . . or write a whole bunch of them and compile an acrostic book. You can even draw illustrations in your book to accompany your acrostics. An acrostic is a poem or series of words written so the first letter of each line or word composes another word. For example:

C olorful
A utomatic
R acing
S leek

F resh
R ipe
U seful
I nviting
T asty

43

CREATE SOME "speaking words." These are words that "do what they say." Some examples are:

disappear   dripping   ST
                               ‾‾   L___ong
                               EP

Si   oo
  n   Candles   j um p   CL⊙CK   TV
   k   j
    i
     ng

What are some "speaking words" you can think of?

MAKE LISTS of your TOP TEN. These can be your TOP TEN favorite foods, singers, songs, television shows, games, Bible heroes, cars, or whatever. Display the lists on your bulletin board or put them in a book.

HOW CAN your beginning writer write without putting pencil to paper? With a homemade print kit. Letter blocks and an ink pad can expand the horizons of your not-so-confident young pencil-pusher.

Materials needed include: plain wooden blocks, one-cubic-inch size; flocked Con-Tact paper; plastic ice-cube tray or egg carton (to store the little blocks in alphabetical order); soap dish with cover; sponge cut to fit soap dish.

1. Draw or trace your letter right on the Con-Tact backing, which is marked into one-inch squares—just the right size!

2. Cut out letters.

3. Peel off backing and stick each letter onto a cube. The letter should be backwards, which will make it right when printed.

4. On the opposite face of the cube copy the letter with a felt pen. In this way you can identify the blocks when the inked side is down.

The best way to be somebody is just to be yourself.

5. Dampen sponge and insert it into the soap dish to make an ink pad.

6. Make "ink" of two parts tempera paint and one part white glue. Apply mixture to ink pad.

7. Print it! Don't expect absolutely "clean" results. Some of the cube may show around the edges of your printed letters.

PREPARE a "mix and match" booklet to inspire your creative writers. Use a two-ring binder or spiral notebook. Cut the sheets of paper in half so that each page has two parts that can be flipped over independently of each other.

When you strike bottom, be of good cheer. Anywhere you go from there is up.

On the top half of each page suggest a character or situation such as, "If I were an astronaut," or "When John was stranded." On the bottom half of each page write a phrase indicating a time or place such as "at the car wash" or "about AD 2004."

Your children can mix and match the phrases and situations until they find one that stirs their imagination and provides a basis for writing a story.

GIVE YOUR children a piece of paper on which you have written a word that can be rhymed with many other words. Let them amuse themselves by filling the page with many rhyming words.

MAKE AN ABC booklet for favorite times of the year. Using magazine cutouts and original drawings, your child can illustrate such topics as "A Spooky ABC," "A Thanksgiving ABC," or "A Wintertime ABC."

HAVE YOUR children look at the headlines on some newspaper stories and then write their own headlines for well-known stories such as the outbreak of the Civil War, Columbus's landing, the first day of school, the discovery of the wheel.

ENCOURAGE creativity. Ask your child to come up with some new ideas such as a new flag or national anthem. Or try making up new endings to old stories. For example, what would have happened if Goldilocks had not run away? Create new holidays. Whose birthdays would you like to celebrate? How?

JUST FOR FUN think of some historical figures and use the person's initial letter to make a whole sentence of words beginning with that letter. For example: "Jefferson juggled Junebugs joyously." or "Franklin fanned funny flames furiously."

One reason so many children are seen on the streets at night is that they are afraid to stay home alone.
—Baltimore News-Post

YOUNG children can write a story about family life by drawing a family portrait. You will discover some fascinating things about how they perceive family relationships (watch for size differences and strange perspectives).

PERHAPS your children would like to concentrate on compiling a family tree. Help them include all their cousins, aunts, uncles, grandparents, brothers, and sisters.

KEEP a record of places that make the news and plot them on a world map. Write a brief paragraph about what happened in each place. Put this on a small piece of paper at the edge of the map and run a piece of yarn from the paragraph to the location of the place.

WRITE "commercials" for some of your favorite foods, toys, cars, etc.

CREATE your own comic strip about happenings in your family.

Definition of TV: radio with eyestrain.

A lot of kneeling keeps you in good standing with God.

MANY children do not understand their parents' occupations. Discuss these with your children. Have them write a story describing your work.

WRITE a story describing what you think the world will be like in ten years . . . in 100 years.

CREATE your own personal code to be used in sending secret messages.

$$A = \odot$$
$$B = \oplus$$
$$C = X$$

MAKE a list of at least 50 things that make you feel good.

PICK AN event in history and write a story pretending "I was there when . . . ."

COMPILE a family history. Write to grandparents and other relatives asking for their help in recalling facts, stories, and events they remember that can be included. Send copies to them when the history is completed.

CREATE your own crossword puzzles.

BEGIN a family project of publishing a monthly family newspaper. Assign various tasks to different family members—reporting, printing, pictures, circulation. Then send the newspaper out to friends and relatives.

Children may tear up a house but they can never break up a home.

LEARN some different types of alphabet. Following are the Viking, Greek, ancient Egyptian hieroglyphics, manual, and braille alphabets.

Viking

A	B	D	F	H	I	K	L

M	N	O	P	R	S	T	U	Y

Greek

A	B	C	D	E	H	I	K	L

M	N	O	P	R	S	T	U

Ancient Egyptian Hieroglyphics

A	B	C	D	E	F	H

I	K	L	M	N	O

P	Q	R	S	T

48

You, O Lord, keep my lamp burning; my God turns my darkness into light. —Psalm 18:28

Manual

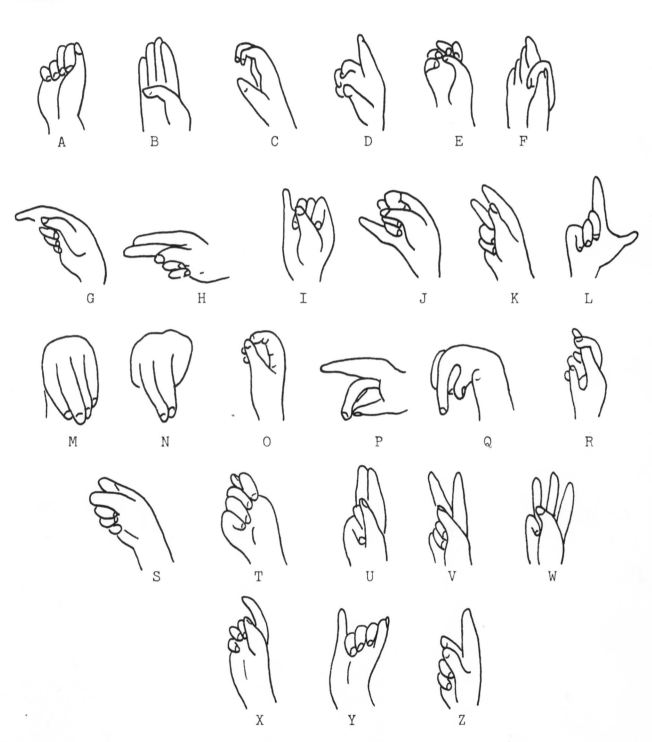

49

Braille

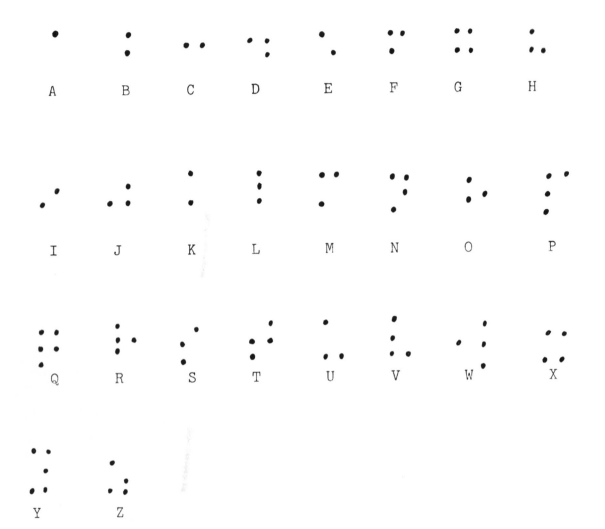

A   B   C   D   E   F   G   H

I   J   K   L   M   N   O   P

Q   R   S   T   U   V   W   X

Y   Z

50

PINS AND NEEDLES, POTS AND PANS

CHAPTER 4

*I will walk in my house
with blameless heart.
—Psalm 101:2*

There is no more important institution than the family. The New Testament gives major attention to the family. Socially, the family is really the first circle of society; all else grows out of it. No nation is stronger or weaker than its family life.

A Christian family submits their lives to Christ; keeps Christ at the center; reads the Bible daily; and expresses their praise and needs together in prayer.

Christian parents can help their children grow up in an atmosphere of love and security in the home. Children need to have a sense of belonging in the family. Tensions will develop in any home, but wise parents resolve them and avoid bickering and quarreling. All this depends upon the attitude of parents. Christian parents enjoy their children and live with them in friendly comradeship and in an atmosphere of reverence for God.

We must never think that because the child is young, his thought processes immature, and his experience and wisdom lacking, that our responsibility is any less. For the child's earliest impressions are the most lasting, and the earliest influences that act upon his life are the most powerful in determining its outcome.

51

Boy, talk about people who don't know their way around a kitchen! I asked for some extract of beef and was served a glass of milk!

Life never stands still—especially the life of a child. It is always advancing, changing, reconstructing. By the time children are three years old they have learned to understand and speak a difficult language. They know the names and uses of hundreds of objects. They recognize dozens of people and have learned to adapt themselves to their ways. They have gained considerable information about every phase of their environment. Their mastery of knowledge is growing rapidly without rest or pause. And the development of attitudes does not lag behind.

In addition to growth in knowledge, specific interests are taking root; ideals are being shaped; standards are developing; enthusiasm is being kindled; loyalties are being formed.

Whether we wish it or not, learning constantly takes place within the family circle. It never ceases. Naturally, easily, and effectively the thinking and living of old and young are shaped by the daily events of homelife. Ideas are fashioned and the emotional quality of the family relationship transforms ideas into prejudices, ideals, and purposes. The cumulative experiences of this intimate group determine lasting attitudes and habits.

In great-grandmother's day family life was close-knit. A home included children of various ages and often two or three generations of adults. They lived, worked, planned, rejoiced, and suffered together. Their home was their world. The economic problem was common to all members of the family and all labored to solve it. Through this labor the children learned valuable attitudes and habits— attitudes and habits which were experienced in practice as well as explained by precept. The learning consisted of experience and interpretation. Attitudes, habits, and religious values were transmitted from the adults to the oncoming generation.

Today most homelife is quite different. Yet we still need to devote our time to teaching children to

There is no verbal vitamin more potent than praise.

care for themselves and for their own families when they are grown. Cooking and sewing skills are some of the most important to learn around the home. To develop such skills, we can take advantage of the natural curiosity and interest that children have concerning these homemaking tasks.

HELP your child understand what is involved in meal planning. Examine the grocery ads in the newspaper. Have your child prepare a shopping list for a meal and determine from the ads just how much the foods will cost.

HOW ABOUT some table setting practice? Colorful place mats with bold outlines of table settings help your child learn where to place the dishes and silverware. Cut paper place mats in half. Outline a toy-size plate, cup, napkin, and eating utensils with a felt pen on the place mat. Let the child use the outlines as a guide for setting the table.

TO DEVELOP the muscles involved in pouring, teach your child to pour rice from a pitcher into a glass. Grasp the pitcher handle with the first two fingers and thumb. Grasp the glass with the other hand. Place the lip of the pitcher opposite the rim of the glass and exactly over its center. Pour from the pitcher into the glass. Repeat until no rice is spilled. Then move on to water-pouring practice.

ALSO teach "control of error"—errors cause spills. You will find much time and energy can be saved if you teach your children to use a sponge to clean up anything they spill.

COLLECT the recipes your children like best and have them draw a picture to go with each recipe. They can then arrange the recipes in a cookbook for their own use in the kitchen.

53

HELP your child become acquainted with a variety of vegetables and how they taste uncooked. Cut them into small finger portions and serve for snacks. Encourage the child to describe the color, texture, and taste as each kind is sampled. You might serve the finger vegetables with cheese or onion dip put in a nut cup. Discuss which part of the vegetable plant we eat and which vegetables are usually cooked before they are eaten.

MAKE A purple cow drink by adding grape juice to a glass of milk.

BANANA CANDY. Break two bananas into one-inch pieces and blend at high speed with two cups raisins until they are well chopped. Scrape into a bowl and allow to sit for a few hours until the mixture can be handled. When dry enough, spoon out bits, shape into one-inch balls, and roll in dry coconut. Makes about 24 candies.

Life is a grindstone. Whether it grinds you down or polishes you up depends on what you're made of.

BUTTER MAKING. Pour several ounces of heavy cream into a jar. Put the lid on tightly. Shake the jar until the cream is churned into butter. Pour off the excess milk. Rinse the butter in cold water. Spread it on crackers and eat! Let your child taste the cream before starting and the no-fat milk that is left over when the butter is finished.

NO-BAKE COOKIES
    ½ cup white corn syrup
    ½ cup peanut butter
    3 cups Rice Krispies cereal
Mix the syrup and peanut butter together. Add the cereal a little at a time. Mix until the cereal is evenly coated. Spoon the mixture onto waxed paper or pat it into an 8 × 8 inch buttered pan. Cut it into squares for serving.

Wife: "Harry! Wake up! I just heard a mouse squeak!"
Husband: "What do you want me to do—get up and oil it?"

SNICKERDOODLES. Mix one-half cup butter, three-quarters cup sugar, and one egg. Sift together 2 cups flour, 1 teaspoon cream of tartar, one-half teaspoon soda, one-eighth teaspoon salt. Stir into first mixture. Roll dough into one-inch balls and roll in cinnamon sugar. Bake on an ungreased baking sheet in a 400° oven for eight minutes or until lightly browned. Makes about 60 cookies.

PAINTED COOKIES. Bake at 375° for 8 minutes. Then paint colorful designs or pictures on them.

1¾ cups sifted all-purpose flour
1¼ teaspoons baking powder
¼ teaspoon salt
½ cup (1 stick) butter or margarine
¾ cup sugar
1 egg
1½ teaspoons vanilla

Sift flour, baking powder, and salt together. Beat butter, sugar, egg, and vanilla in medium-sized bowl with electric mixer until fluffy. Gradually stir in flour mixture at low speed or with a wooden spoon until dough is very stiff. If needed, stir in more flour. Dough can be chilled overnight.

Roll out dough, one half at a time, between a lightly floured sheet of foil and a sheet of waxed paper, to a ⅛-inch thickness, lifting paper frequently to dust with flour and turning dough over for even rolling. Remove waxed paper. Cut dough with floured 3-inch cutter, leaving ½-inch between cookies. Remove dough trimmings from foil. Place foil with cut-out dough on cookie sheet. Bake. Remove foil to wire racks; cool cookies completely. Remove from foil and paint.

The paint is made from egg yolks. Mix an egg yolk with a little water and divide it into two or three small bowls. Add a few drops of food coloring to each bowl and stir. Use a small, clean paintbrush to do the decorating.

THE HOUSEWIFE
Jesus, teach me how to be
Pleased with my sim-
plicity.
Sweep the floors, wash
the clothes,
Gather for each vase a
rose.
Iron and mend a tiny
frock,
Taking notice of the
clock.
Always having time kept
free
For childish questions
asked of me.
Grant me wisdom Mary
had
When she taught her
little Lad.
—Coblentz

MAKE your own magazine dinner. Cut pictures of food from magazines or newspapers. Put the pictures on a table and pretend you are serving the foods. What utensils would you need to serve and eat the different foods?

I know a woman who has cooked so many TV dinners she thinks she's in show business.

WHEN carving a jack-o'-lantern, save the seeds. Spread them on a cookie sheet and sprinkle with salt. Bake in a 350° oven for about 15 minutes until brown. Cool and eat.

CHOCOLATE WORMS
1 bag chocolate chips
2 cans chow mein noodles

Melt chocolate chips in an electric fry pan; then stir in the noodles. Drop by teaspoon onto waxed paper and refrigerate.

ANTS ON A LOG
celery sticks
softened cream cheese or
    peanut butter
raisins

Wash and dry the celery. Cut the stalks into 1½ inch pieces. Fill these with cream cheese or peanut butter and top them off with a few raisins on each piece. A great picnic snack!

FLOWER POT BREADS
1 pkg. yeast
3 cups water
dash salt
1 teaspoon sugar
3 cups flour

Among those things that are so simple that even a child can operate are parents.

Dissolve yeast in 1 cup warm water. Add salt, sugar, and ½ cup flour. Add another ½ cup flour and set aside for 30 minutes. Mix together remaining 2 cups of water and remaining 2 cups of flour and add yeast mixture. Let rise for one hour. Pour into greased and floured 3-inch diameter clay flower pots (fill about ¾ full). Bake at 350° for one hour.

ENERGY NOG

1 cup orange juice
1 tablespoon honey
1 egg
2 ice cubes

Mix all the ingredients in a blender until frothy. A nutritious snack.

POPOVERS

1 cup flour
¼ teaspoon salt
2 eggs well-beaten
1 cup milk
½ teaspoon melted butter

Mix salt and flour; then add eggs, milk, and butter. Pour into lightly greased muffin tins and bake for 30 minutes at 450°. great for popovers

GRANOLA

3 cups rolled oats
1/3 cup brown sugar
½ teaspoon salt
½ cup vegetable oil
1 cup dried apple slices
1/3 cup pumpkin seeds
1 cup raisins
½ cup walnuts
1/3 cup shelled
sunflower seeds
2 tablespoons
sesame seeds

Combine rolled oats, brown sugar, salt, and oil in a large bowl. Add apples, raisins, walnuts, sunflower seeds, pumpkin seeds, and sesame seeds to oat mixture, stirring thoroughly. Spread mixture in a 15 x 10 x 1-inch jelly-roll pan. Bake in a slow oven (300°) for 20 minutes, turning once. Remove to wire rack. Cool thoroughly. Store in a tightly covered container.

PARTY FOODS. Turn an ice-cream cone (with a scoop of ice cream in it) upside down for a clown.

Fill a tiny flower pot or paper cup with ice cream and top it with a lollipop to make a flower.

Create animals with toothpicks, marshmallows, and gumdrops.

CINNAMON TOAST. Mix together in a cup: 1 teaspoon cinnamon and 2 tablespoons sugar. Make two pieces of toast. Butter it while hot. Sprinkle with the cinnamon mix and eat it while it's still warm.

It takes a heap o' livin' in a house t' make it a home.
—Edgar A. Guest

APPLESAUCE WITH SOUR CREAM. Put two 8-ounce cans of applesauce into a big mixing bowl. Add 1 tablespoon brown sugar, ½ cup sour cream, and 1 teaspoon lemon juice and mix well. Refrigerate for at least one hour. Serve in dessert bowls.

SEW buttons onto a piece of material in the form of a design or picture. Then frame the work of art.

TO TEACH basic sewing, help your child thread a needle and tie a knot in the thread. Let him or her sew together scraps of material for practice.

Mother: "Why did you fall in the mud puddle with your new dress on?"
Sally: "There wasn't time to take it off!"

ANOTHER good way to teach beginning stitchery is to put a piece of burlap in an embroidery hoop. Use large plastic needles and colorful yarn. You can outline a picture on the burlap with a felt pen. Your child can stitch the yarn following the lines of your picture.

58

BELT BRAIDING. Use heavy twine or lengths of material. Measure the length around your child's waist and add about 12 inches. Cut the twine or material to that length. Then use that piece to measure two more strips. Show your child how to take the three strands and braid them to make a belt. Tie a knot at each end.

MOCK STITCHERY. Cover a large board with fabric such as burlap, felt, or corduroy. Plan your design—something simple such as birds, flowers, or animals. Draw the design on the fabric with a felt pen, blocking in areas for different colors. Choose your colors in inexpensive cotton rug yarns. Apply white glue to one color area. Starting from the outside of this area, press a strand of yarn around so it fills it with a swirl of yarn. Clip the yarn at the center of the swirl. Go on to another color. Finally, outline all color sections with black yarn. This pushes the design forward and creates an effective wall hanging.

RUG BRAIDING. Braided scraps of material can be turned into decorative rugs. Cut old towels, colored sheets, or other material into strips just long enough to work with. Braid them together, sewing new strips onto the ends as you get to them. When you have several feet braided, begin winding it together to form a rug. Sew the rows together.

STITCHERY can be a difficult project to introduce to young children. Perhaps this project will help make it a bit easier. Obtain a piece of screen wire about 9 x 12 inches in size. Tape around the edges to keep the sharp wires from scratching your child. Put yarn in a large plastic needle and let the child stitch in and out the holes in the screen wire. After mastering the simple stitches, the child can progress to creating interesting designs. These can be framed for hanging.

BURLAP is a unique fabric to work with. By pulling some of the threads you can create interesting designs in the material. These holes can be filled by weaving into them an assortment of twigs, dried flowers, and grasses, or just about anything else. Exciting wall hangings can be made by pulling out some of the threads to create holes, stitching a yarn design on part of the burlap, then gluing wooden beads in other places on the burlap.

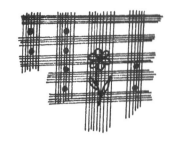

WEAVING can be done by using a coat hanger for a loom. Bend the hanger into an interesting shape and straighten out the hook and insert it into a piece of board for a stand. Tie a piece of yarn at the top of the "sculpture" and wind it around and around from one side to the other; then tie it at that end. The weaving is then done by tying other pieces of yarn to one end and weaving it in and out of the other yarn until you reach the other end where it is then tied to the hanger. Continue this procedure until you have completed your design.

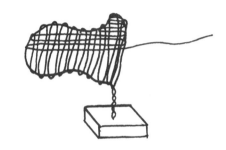

BASKET WEAVING is a craft that can utilize recycled cottage cheese cartons and yarn. Cut down the sides of the carton to make an odd number of sections. A handle can be cut from cardboard and glued to the carton. Now tie the end of a skein of yarn about the base of one of the sections, knotting it on the inside, and begin to weave it in and out of the sections. Push the yarn all the way down. Continue in this manner as long as you want to use that particular color. When a new color is started, tie off the preceding color and knot the new one inside the container as before. Weave the colors until the entire container is covered. Then finish wrapping the handle.

*If fate throws a dagger at
   you
Catch it by the handle,
   not the blade.
If you get a lemon in life,
   Make lemonade.*

*Helen Keller did. John
Bunyan did. Adoniram
Judson did. Probably we
all know someone who
has made lemonade from
the lemons of life.*

DOLL CLOTHES, carpenter and kitchen aprons, scarves and costumes can be made by children from scrap material. The patterns can be easily designed, many using just squares of material sewn together. Coloring books can often provide the basic picture for making a design. Just enlarge the picture a bit to allow for seams.

VELCRO, which can be obtained at notions counters, can be used for fastening garments rather than using buttons or snaps.

EMBROIDERY is fast becoming an important pastime for both boys and girls and is being taught in many schools. You can make your own patterns by tracing pictures from coloring books. Then all you need is some plain-colored material, an em-broidery hoop, needle, and thread—and you can make many useful and decorative items.

A TUNE, A TURN, AND A TWIST

CHAPTER 5

Be careful to obey all these regulations I am giving you, so that it may always go well with you and your children after you, because you will be doing what is good and right in the eyes of the Lord your God.
—Deuteronomy 12:28

Children need guidance in developing avenues of interest, creativity, and expression. This involves encouraging them to devote themselves wholeheartedly to whatever they feel at any one time is worth more than anything else in their world. At the same time we must prepare them for progression when a still more worthy object emerges to take the crowning place in their world of values. One of the most difficult things for the adult is to have a genuine and adequate regard for the objectives of interest chosen by small children. Their objectives are bound to seem trivial and transitory compared with those which we in our almost infinite wisdom would advocate!

It is precariously easy for an adult to crush the tender outthrusting of a new interest in a child. All it may take is one unmistakable evidence of amused superiority, impatient disdain, bored tolerance, disparagement, ridicule, or sarcasm to wither it forever. On the other hand, it requires little effort, many times, to provide a beneficial climate for the germinating and sprouting of a genuine, if seemingly small, growth in interests.

There are several ways of changing the emphasis in the interest of children. One of the strongest ones, particularly during the earlier years, is the natural sharing with them of adult enthusiasm for certain forms of satisfaction. A child tends to think, "If daddy likes it as much as that, there must be something to it." Another helpful exercise is to sustain or repeat some particular situation in which children are experiencing new interests until they have given the activity a fair chance.

Music, drama, and physical movement are forms of expression and creativity which contribute immensely to the growth of children. Each of these interests contains self-disciplines which will prepare them for their years in school and ultimately in the work force.

So many children spend their hours sitting in front of a television set that self-expression and creativity are severely stifled. According to one estimate, children watch 22,000 hours of television between kindergarten and grade 12. During the same years they only spend 11,000 hours in school. However, we can turn some of these TV hours into expressive opportunities by encouraging children to use this time investment wisely. Help them to watch worthwhile programs. Keep a list posted on a bulletin board or the refrigerator of suitable programs to view. Then transform passive watchers into active critics in family discussion groups about the programs. Here is a list of "feeling" words for children to use in describing TV scenes and how they make them feel: relieved, frightened, disappointed, very happy, excited, worried, frustrated, nervous, grief-stricken, shocked, sad, confused, tense, or like laughing or crying. Talk about the program and determine if it is worth watching again. Does it elicit an emotional response that is beneficial?

Music can set a mood or create atmosphere. Play different types of music and discuss with the children how it makes them feel. Also, singing gives

Do not merely listen to the word, and so deceive yourselves. Do what it says.   —James 1:22

children the chance to develop their ear and their pitch, both of which will help them appreciate music.

Block buildings have to be torn down and paintings eventually dry or tear, but children will remember for many years the songs they have learned.

Children enjoy spontaneous singing. They don't care whether it is special singing time or not. They sing songs that they know, or they make up songs of their own. By taking these songs seriously, you encourage further musical experimentation.

The rhythm of a piece of music is the first thing children respond to. Using rhythm instruments they can experiment with the beat of a piece of music and the various kinds of sounds that instruments make. Even clapping hands and stamping feet can be used as rhythm instruments.

Drama is a most useful medium of expression. By providing opportunities for dramatic play, we allow children freedom to express their innermost thoughts. This can be helpful in determining if they are developing correct concepts of life. We can learn their thoughts, their language, their interpretation of family life, social interactions, and religion. From this we will know how to work with them to correct any misconceptions. Dress-up play and puppetry are two forms of drama that are easily achieved by every child.

Various body movements are also forms of creative expression as well as avenues for release of pent-up energy. Moving like a certain animal or pretending one is walking through a cloud are expressions of how the child "feels" about the animal or the cloud. Body movement or exercise also helps teach children awareness of themselves as persons and increases their ability to make their bodies perform as they wish. It also provides a good teaching opportunity for helping the child relate to God, the one who created arms and legs, eyes and

If I am out of TUNE with myself and have DISCORD with my neighbors, how can I expect to be in HARMONY with God?

ears, a mouth, hands and feet to do these things. You can help children think of their bodies as God's temple and encourage them to keep them clean, in shape, and free from harmful drugs.

Gradually during their early years children should be forming a clear concept of religion and the part it is to play in their lives. This cannot come through any formal definition, nor through any set of precepts. It must be a growth process, stimulated by instruction, guided by wise counsel, given depth of meaning through the lives of strong men and women who express the Christian ideal in their daily living.

Reach up as far as you can; God will reach down all the rest of the way.

A "FOOTPRINT" activity will help your child release energy and relax tired muscles. Cut outlines of a child's shoe from two different colors of cardboard or paper: one color for the right foot, another color for the left. Use masking tape to fasten the outlines to the floor in either a circular path or in a straight line. Your child can hop from one footprint to another. Vary the activity by telling her (or him) to hop on her left foot on all the left footprints; on her right foot on all the right footprints. She can say "left" and "right" each time she steps on the correct footprint.

KEEP your legs straight and without bending your knees try to do the following: march around the room, bend and touch your toes, jump up and down.

FOLD both arms behind your back, clasping your elbows, and do the following: walk a straight line, alternate stooping and standing, step over three stacks of objects placed about a foot apart in a row.

PRETEND you are an elephant! Fasten your hands together in front of you to make the elephant's trunk. Bend over slightly, swinging your "trunk" from side to side as you march around the room. Put on a record or some music from the radio that you can march with. Different types of music might inspire you to become other animals . . . a rabbit, a duck, a penguin, a monkey. What would a fish do?

COMBINE imagination with coordination. Make a "tightrope" on the floor with masking tape. Perform a balancing act while on the "tightrope."

FOR a fast-paced exercise to increase bodily awareness, chant the following verses: "Head, shoulders, knees and toes/Knees and toes/Head, shoulders, knees and toes/Knees and toes/Eyes and ears and mouth and nose/Mouth and nose/ Eyes and ears and mouth and nose/Mouth and nose. As you name each part of the body touch it. See how fast you can go.

Dr. Karl Menninger was asked at a forum once what one should do if he felt a nervous breakdown coming on. The famous psychiatrist said, "If you feel a nervous breakdown coming on, lock up your house, go across the railroad tracks, find someone in need, and do something for him."

TRY THESE EXERCISES:
Here we go, up, up, up (reach up high)
Here we go, down, down, down (stoop/ touch floor)
Here we go, backward and forward (bend back and forth)
And here we go, around and around (turn around)

Let's play rag doll.
Don't make a sound.
Fling your arms and bodies
Loosely around.
Fling your hands—fling your feet,
Let your hands go free.
Be the raggiest rag doll
You ever did see.

66

MOVE in different ways while singing the following verses to the tune of "Mary Had a Little Lamb."

I will walk around the room, around the
room, around the room,
I will walk around the room, come and walk
with me.
I will hop around the room, etc.
I will fly around the room, etc.
I will run on tiptoe now, etc.

Living without faith is like driving in the fog.

BECOME more aware of controlling movement of different parts of the body by doing the following exercises while singing the words to the tune of "Mulberry Bush."

Point to your knees and make them bend,
make them bend, make them bend,
Point to your knees and make them bend,
make them bend just so.

Point to your head and make it nod, etc.
Point to your eyes and make them blink, etc.
Point to your lips and make them smack, etc.
Point to your shoulders and make them
drop, etc.
Point to your foot and make it shake, etc.
Lift your hands and make them clap, etc.

GIVE your child an inflated balloon and let him try to do the following:
—Keep the ballon in the air using only his
head, shoulders, knees, feet,
etc. . . . no hands.
—Toss the balloon in the air and clap three
times before catching it again.
—Toss the balloon in the air, then touch his
nose and toes before catching it again.

HOW does different music make you feel? Listen to various types of music from records or the radio. Which music sounds happy? Which is sad? How would you walk if you were happy? Sad? Big and heavy as an elephant? Light as a spider? Is there big elephant music? Quick spider music?

If you were another person, would you like to be your friend?

MAKE some rhythm instruments. Here are directions for several. Perhaps you can invent some of your own.

A drum can be made from round oatmeal boxes painted or covered with colored paper and decorated. Or the plastic top may be taped on an empty coffee can and Con-Tact paper put around the can for decoration.

Glue coarse sandpaper to blocks of wood. Rub them together to make a scraping sound.

Attach bells to a heavy string or yarn. Tie the string in a circle large enough to slip over your hand. Clap your hands together to make the bells ring.

Materials such as buttons, macaroni, dry beans, or peas may be placed in small boxes or Band-Aid cans. These can be decorated and used as rattles.

To make rhythm sticks, sand and paint wooden dowels. Twelve-inch lengths of one-half inch doweling are adequate.

Remove the cork liners from bottle caps. Punch a hole in each cap. Punch holes in the rim of a foil pie pan. Tie the caps to the rim of the pie pan with heavy string and you will have a good tambourine.

Bend round curtain rods or coat hangers into triangles. Tie pieces of heavy string to the top of the triangles. Hold the triangles by the string and hit them with old spoons.

Use two coconut halves to make interesting

sounds when hitting them together or hitting them on a piece of wood.

Fill glasses with varying amounts of water. Strike the glasses lightly at the top to hear the different sounds. Arrange the glasses in order from high note to low note. See if you can play the scale. What songs can you play on the musical glasses?

Tell the child about David playing a harp while he watched sheep on the hills around Bethlehem. Then make a simple harp together. Here are the directions. Bend a piece of wire (a coat hanger will do fine) into the following shape:

Tie narrow elastic cord to the wire and tape it with masking tape all around the wire. You can also use rubber bands. Pluck the strings and play a song!

No matter what your lot in life, be sure to build something on it.

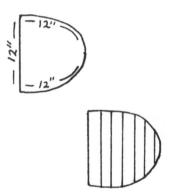

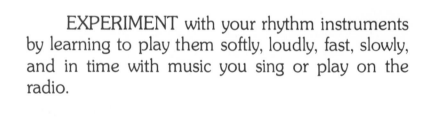

EXPERIMENT with your rhythm instruments by learning to play them softly, loudly, fast, slowly, and in time with music you sing or play on the radio.

TAKE a big cardboard tube from a paper towel roll. Punch a row of four or five holes with a pencil. Make sure the holes are nice and round. Now cut a piece of waxed paper the right size to fit over one end of the tube. Fasten it with a rubber band. Hum into the open end of the tube. Put your fingers over the holes and lift them one at a time to make different notes. What kind of music can you play on your HUMBUZZER? Soft? Loud? Fast? Slow?

LEARN A SONG in a different language. Here are the words to "Jesus Loves the Little Children" in several languages. (If possible, check the correct pronounciation with a person who is acquainted with the language.)

English:

> Jesus loves the little children
> All the children of the world.
> Red or yellow, black or white,
> All are precious in his sight.
> Jesus loves the little children of the world.

French:

> Jesu aime les petits enfants
> Tous les enfants de la monde.
> Rouge et jaune, noir et blanc,
> Ils sont precieux dans sa vision.
> Jesu aime les petits enfants de la monde.

Hispanic:

> Jesus ama les niñitos del mundo
> Todos les niñitos del mundo.
> Rajo, yamarillo, negro y blanco,
> Son preciosos en sus ojos.
> Jesus ama les niñitos del mundo.

Here are the words to "Yes, Jesus Loves Me."

English:

> Yes, Jesus loves me!
> Yes, Jesus loves me!
> Yes, Jesus loves me!
> The Bible tells me so.

Worry is like a rocking chair—it gives you something to do, but it won't get you anywhere.

Chinese:

> Ju Ye-su ai wo!
> Ju Ye-su ai wo!
> Ju Ye-su ai wo!
> Shung jing i ko-ru wo.

Formosan:

> Si, la-so thia goa!
> Si, la-so thia goa!
> Si, la-so thia goa!
> U ki-chai ti Seng-keng.

70

WRITE new words for one of your favorite songs. The tune is already there, just waiting for a new story to accompany it.

When you're through changing, you're through!

HELP teach sound discrimination. Have the children follow your hand movement with their voices. For instance, when you raise your hand, their voices will get softer. When you lower your hand, their voices will get louder. Move your hand all the way up and down as the children sing along. Then move your hand only part way up and down.

KEEP an "old clothes" box available for dress-up play. Shirts, scarves, hats, shoes, skirts, jewelry, and gloves present opportunities for dramatic or interpretive play which is beneficial to young children.

FROM a damaged or old copy of a book cut the pictures of characters and paste them on popsicle sticks to make stick puppets.

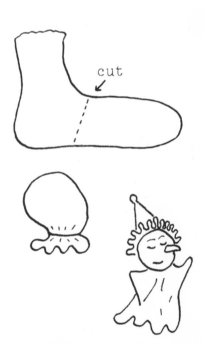

cut

SOCK PUPPETS are interesting and fun to make. Cut a sock about three inches from the toe. Stuff the toe with cotton or soft scrap cloth. Then tie the opening. This becomes the puppet's head. Leave just enough room for your finger to push in and move the head about. Now drape a piece of cloth around the "neck" of your puppet for its clothing and to hide your hand when using the puppet. Give your puppet a personality by painting on a face. Glue yarn on for hair.

EXPERIMENT with making sound effects for dramas or puppet plays. Crumple paper for the sound of fire, hit a cookie sheet for the sound of thunder, rub sandpaper together, tear cloth, wind a clock. What other sounds can you make?

USE AN OLD window shade for a puppet theater. Put the hanging brackets in a doorway then just hang the shade when you want to use the puppet theater. It can be rolled up and put away when not in use. Decorate the shade to look like a stage. Cut a slit to allow the puppets to come from behind the stage to do their acting.

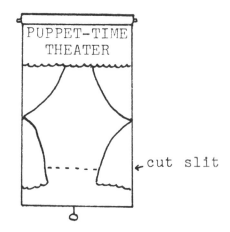

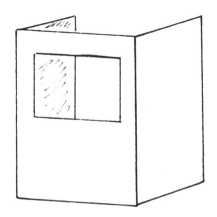

CUT three panels of corrugated cardboard to make another type of puppet stage. A refrigerator or TV packing box is good for this. Tape the panels together so you have a trifold standing theater. Cut an opening near the top of the front panel. A curtain may be hung over the opening to hide the backstage activity.

FINGER PUPPETS are the easiest kind to make. Use a picture of a person or animal about 1½ inches high and 2½ inches wide. Make a ring from heavy paper about 1½ inches wide by 1 inch high. With paste or Scotch tape close the ring so it fits on your finger. Paste the figure to the ring. Slip the ring on your finger and you are ready to perform with your puppet.

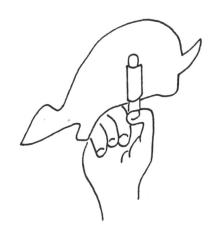

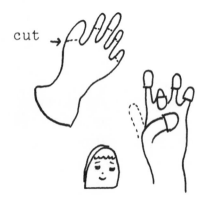

GATHER old white cotton gloves. Draw faces on the finger tips of the gloves. Glue yarn on for hair. Felt scraps can be made into hats. Cut the ends of the glove fingers off about one to three-fourths inch from the tip. These will fit on your fingers to make five puppets. Move your fingers as the different puppets speak. The fingers can be folded into the palm then raised as the puppets take turns speaking.

However, as it is written:
"No eye has seen,
no ear has heard,
no mind has conceived
what God has prepared
for those
who love him."
    —1 Corinthians 2:9

DRAW FACES on wooden picnic spoons to create little puppets. You can glue on yarn and pieces of fabric to make hair, bow ties, etc., on them.

Patterns for hand puppets and marionettes are included in chapter 10.

EXPLORING, EXPERIMENTING, AND EXPERIENCING EARTH'S EXCITING EXISTENCE

CHAPTER 6

*There is a time for
    everything . . .
a time to be born and a
    time to die,
a time to plant and a time
    to uproot . . .
a time to weep and a time
    to laugh . . .
a time to keep and a time
    to throw away . . .
a time to be silent and a
    time to speak.
        —Ecclesiastes 3:1-7*

There are many things which bewilder young children. They sense elements in the world-within-their-reach which are strange, fascinating, inconsistent, evil, glamorous, confusing, enticing, threatening, awesome, seemingly unconquerable. Since they are new in a world that is always both very old and very new, it is not surprising that they are frequently puzzled or frightened.

Many adults feel flattered when children cling to the familiar. Yet if children are to achieve rich fulfillment of life, they will have to learn how to deal with the unfamiliar, and how to discern in all their experiences the important connections which lead to further exploration of the unfamiliar.

Interpretation of the unfamiliar in specific experiences involves helping children locate what elements are known to them and how to approach the unknown elements from these knowns. It is a matter of making them keen and skilled explorers. Children can be led to regard the unfamiliar as an unexplored realm of possibilities.

We are not striving, through the teaching of

science, to raise a new generation of scientists; but we are trying to rear young men and women who will have respect for the creations of God and who will love him and be drawn closer to him through their knowledge of his wonderful world.

Children whose special work in life is yet un-chosen should be helped to realize that in some future work they will need the completest possible discipline of all their powers to attain their highest goals. Now is the time to get ready.

Happiness, like pure gold, is rarely found in huge nuggets but is scattered in precious particles through the common rock of daily living. It is only when we gather these shining bits together that we realize how rich we are in joy.

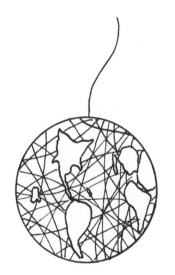

STRING GLOBE. Make geography come alive for your child. Using a cup of liquid starch, a small round balloon, a piece of string, and about 20 strips of 19-inch long blue yarn, you can construct an unusual hanging globe.

Inflate the balloon and tie the end. Then dip the yarn pieces in the starch and crisscross them around the balloon in all directions. When the balloon is almost completely covered with yarn, there will still be small spaces left between the intersecting lines. Hang the balloon overnight so that the yarn can dry and stiffen. In the morning break the balloon with a pin and gently pull it out through one of the spaces between the strips of yarn. Now obtain a large world map and either trace the different continents on another sheet of paper or cut them out of the map.

Carefully glue the continents where they belong on the yarn globe. The names of countries, cities, locations of major mountains, lakes, and rivers can be drawn on the cutout continents with crayons or felt pens. The blue yarn will be the oceans. Hang the globe from the ceiling to help your child understand the locations, shapes, and sizes of the world's continents.

MAGNET MANEUVERS. Draw a simple maze on an eight-inch cardboard square. Have the child place a paper clip at the start of the maze and, holding the card in one hand, manipulate a magnet under the card to pull the paper clip through the maze.

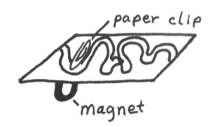

paper clip

magnet

Little Mary was visiting her grandmother in the country. Walking in the garden, Mary saw a peacock, a bird she had never seen before. After gazing in silent admiration, she ran into the house and cried out: "Oh, granny, come and see! One of your chickens is in bloom!"

SPONGES can be lots of fun. Using scissors, cut out small pieces of thin sponge in the shape of various letters or animals. You don't have to be an artist to do this, as many animals have simple outlines. For example, owls, fish, butterflies, and turtles are easy to make. After you have cut out several sponge figures, dip them in water to wet them. Then wad each one up tightly and wrap a rubber band around it, or slip it between a paper clip. Now either freeze the sponges or let them dry. If the sponge is the type that is soft and flexible when dry, you will have to freeze your wadded-up figures. Freezing should take about an hour. After the sponges are frozen, remove the rubber bands or paper clips. Drop the wadded-up sponges into a pan of water and they will slowly unfold. Try to guess the letter or animal before the sponge is completely unfolded.

EARLY in the morning, if possible, suggest that your child collect items that can be soaked with water, such as a cloth scrap, a piece of paper, a glass, etc. The objects should be thoroughly wet and set aside where they won't be touched. Then have the child predict which item will dry first and why. Check the objects periodically to observe the drying process. How close were the child's predictions to the actual outcome?

EXAMINE a thermometer with your child, demonstrating that warm hands, snow, or a piece of ice will change the red line. By this activity help the child understand that there are dependable ways of knowing when wraps are needed to keep us warm when the temperature is cold.

EXPERIMENT with dew drops with this simple procedure. All you need are a large funnel and a clean, dry, empty bottle to put the funnel in. Set the bottle outside overnight. As dew forms during the night it will collect on the funnel, condense, and drip into the bottle. Do this each day for a week. When you check the bottle each morning you will see how much water collected from the overnight dew. Note which days bring heavy concentrations of dew and which ones bring less. You'll discover that a combination of lower temperatures and higher humidity during the day causes more dew to collect.

Some people ask the Lord to direct them and then grab the steering wheel.
—Smeltzer

WATCH "flowers" grow from a lump of coal. Use the following activity as a science project on crystal formation or a visual experience in shape and color. Put a few lumps of soft coal, coke, porous brick, tile, cement, or sponge in a glass bowl. Over these, pour two tablespoons each of water, table salt, and liquid blueing. The next morning add two more tablespoons of salt. On the third morning pour into the bottom of the bowl two tablespoons each of salt, water, and blueing. Then add a drop or two of Mercurochrome, vegetable coloring, or stamp pad ink to each lump. Do not use iodine.

By now a flowerlike growth should appear. Circulating air is necessary and the formations will develop better if the air is also dry. To keep the "flowers" growing, just add more blueing, salt, and water from time to time.

SPIDERWEBS can be collected to study by a simple procedure. When you see a spiderweb on a tree or fence spray it with spray paint. Then slip a piece of paper (contrasting color to that of the paint used) behind it, draw the paper slowly toward the web until the web is "captured" by the paper. The paint will cause the web to stick to the paper. These can be framed and hung for display.

HOW DOES your garden grow? Watch the growing process for yourself with a miniature plastic-bag greenhouse. Materials for the individual seedbeds are: Ziploc plastic bags, paper towels, and some large quick-sprouting seeds such as radish, peas, or beans. Plant the garden by following these steps: (1) in each bag place a damp paper towel; (2) put some seeds into each bag—various kinds in separate rows or different kinds in different bags—and lock the bags; (3) arrange the bags on a shelf or in several shallow boxes and begin your observation.

Check the seeds daily to see which ones sprout first and keep a record of how fast they grow. There's no need to rewater the toweling. If the bags are locked shut, the toweling will stay moist and the seeds will grow in about three weeks. After the seeds have grown about three inches tall, they can be transplanted outdoors or in indoor planters.

We never know what ripples of healing we set in motion by simply smiling on one another.
—Henry Drummond

Tape on un-ripe apple

LET'S PAINT apples with the sun! The sun is like a big brush that paints—not on paper—but on plants. The sun helps turn green leaves to red or yellow in the fall. And the sun paints many fruits a different color when they are ripe. The sun turns apples red when they are ripe, but only the side that is in the sun. The shaded side may still be yellow or green. But if you set the shaded side in the sun, it too will turn red. Go to the store and purchase a red apple that is still partly green. (Don't get a yellow apple that is not supposed to turn red.) Then cut from heavy paper the letters of your name or a simple picture such as a star or simple animal. Put the letters or picture on a piece of cellophane tape and stick the tape to the green side of the apple. Set the apple in a window so the sun will shine where the tape is. In a few days the green side will turn red. Remove the tape and you will see your name or the picture is still green. The sun has painted the apple, except where it could not reach it under the letters.

Tape off ripe apple

STATIC electricity is interesting to watch. Obtain a box with a plastic lid, puffed rice, tissue paper, a piece of wool cloth, and an inflated balloon. Place a handful of puffed rice and bits of tissue in the box with a plastic lid. Rub the plastic with your hand or a piece of wool and watch the objects dance in the box and cling to the lid.

Rub the balloon against your clothing or hair. Touch it to the wall and watch it stick. Hold the balloon over your head and you'll look like you've seen a ghost—your hair will stand on end!

Charge a comb by rubbing it on something made of wool. Now cut some pieces of nylon, silk, or cotton thread. Make some of the threads short, some long. Move the comb near the threads. They'll dance like charmed snakes.

The heavens declare the glory of God; the skies proclaim the work of his hands.   —Psalm 19:1

TOUCH-N-FEEL books or pictures are fun. Either secure pictures of animals from magazines or make them by tracing pictures from a coloring book. Glue or paste on them things that will add texture to the animals, such as cotton on lambs and rabbits, fake fur on tigers, bears, or cats, dried peas cut in half for a turtle's shell, feathers on birds, etc.

MAKE a rainbow. All you need is a glass of water and a sunny day. Be sure to use a clear glass. The wider the mouth, the better. When you place the glass in sunlight, look for a rainbow where the shadow would fall. What you have made is a simple prism which reflects the color spectrum. A rainbow forms outdoors when drops of water in the air act as prisms. What Bible story do you know that tells about a rainbow? Read Genesis 6 to 9.

DRINKING PLANTS. Fill a glass with water and add red food coloring. Cut the bottom off a carrot and a stalk of celery and place them in the water. Let them stand for several hours, then cut them open. What happened?

COLORED LENSES add new interest to the familiar things in a child's world. To make a colored lens, obtain bright-colored cellophane paper and cut it into a five-inch square. Glue four popsicle sticks along the outer edge of the cellophane square, both front and back. Allow it to dry thoroughly, then glue another stick on for a handle. Now hold up the lens and look out the window. What color is the sky? The tree? What colors have changed inside the house?

Art is man's nature; nature is God's art.

Most of the folks I know who have good luck seem to have good judgment, too.

BALLOON MAGIC. Baking soda is a solid. Vinegar is a liquid. When you mix them, what do you get? A gas—carbon dioxide. You can see it happen in this experiment. Put two teaspoons of baking soda into an empty balloon. Then put one inch of vinegar into an empty soda pop bottle. Fit the neck of the balloon tightly over the neck of the bottle. Shake the soda from the balloon into the bottle. Watch closely. In a few seconds—like magic—the balloon will begin to expand. The soda and vinegar have formed carbon dioxide gas, and this gas is filling the balloon.

U.S. astronauts returned home with 96 pounds of rocks and dirt. But a mother claims her first-grade son still holds the record. —*Knoxville News Sentinel*

WEATHER WATCH. Each day mark symbols and words on a calendar to describe the day's weather. Use this calendar to reinforce counting and number skills. Ask how many cloudy, rainy, sunny, and windy days there were during the week. During the month. Which week had the most sunny days?

FASTEN A BIRD feeder outside the window. The flutter of wings and chirping will soon catch the attention of your child. String berries or popcorn to hang on the feeder or put bird seed mixed in peanut butter on a pinecone. How many different kinds of birds came to your feeder? Remind the child that God gave us many pretty birds to help make our world a beautiful place to live.

MOTHER NATURE PRESERVES. One way to save those souvenirs from field and forest is to put them under glass. Use clear glass jars with screw-on tops. A late fall walk can yield a wide variety of dried plants, seeds, seed pods, nuts, burrs, twigs, bark, etc. Put some modeling clay on the inside of the jar lid. Be sure not to spread the clay too close to the edge of the lid. There must be room to put it back on the jar later. Arrange the plants and other items in the clay to create a nature scene. Miniature ceramic or plastic animals can be added to the scene. Place the jar carefully over the arrangement and tighten the cover. This arrangement will last a long time if kept airtight.

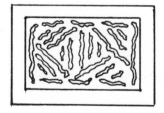

WINTER is full of sticks. Collect a good variety of sizes and shapes. Dip the sticks in paste or glue and attach them to a piece of cardboard to make a stick collage. When the glue dries, the sticks may be painted.

Middle age is when the narrow waist and the broad mind begin to change places.

PRESERVING LEAVES. Collect different kinds of leaves for these projects. To make leaf casts you will need nonhardening clay and plaster of paris. Flatten the clay with a rolling pin and arrange a leaf on top. Move the rolling pin over the leaf. Carefully remove the leaf and you will see its impression in the clay. Surround the impression with a circlet of cardboard one to two inches high. Press the cardboard slightly into the clay to make it stand and close the circle with a paper clip. Mix some plaster of paris and pour it into this "mold." When the plaster has hardened, remove the cardboard and clay. The plaster cast can now be painted.

Use a piece of flat crayon to make a leaf print. Place the leaf on a cushion of folded newspaper and cover it with a sheet of construction paper. Hold the leaf firmly in place and rub the crayon across it, stroking in one direction only. A detailed print will soon emerge.

Use an ink pad to make an ink print. The leaf is placed on the pad with its veins down and is covered with a piece of newspaper. The paper is then gently rubbed until one side of the leaf is fully inked. Next, the leaf is transferred to a sheet of blank paper. It is once again covered (to keep ink off your hands) with newspaper and rubbed. Remove the newspaper and the leaf to see your leaf print.

Create a leaf puppet by drawing a face on a leaf with a felt pen.

Iron several leaves between two pieces of waxed paper and hang it in front of a window. Place the waxed paper between sheets of newspaper before ironing with low heat.

WORM HOUSE. In a large clear glass jar or goldfish bowl place the following in layers: soil, tree leaves, cabbage leaves, coffee grounds, ½ teaspoon brown sugar. Finish with a thin layer of soil on top, then place a few earthworms on top of the soil. Sprinkle a little water on top. Cover the sides of the jar with dark paper to keep light from them. After a few days take the paper off and observe what has happened. The worms will have made tunnels through the mixture. Some of the tunnels may be visible along the sides of the jar. Add a little water, brown sugar, and cabbage leaves periodically. Keep the dark paper on the sides of the jar except when you are observing the worms.

Not having prayers in schools shouldn't worry us as much as not having prayers in homes.

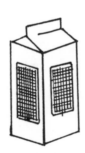

INSECT HOUSES. Collect a variety of insects such as ladybugs, caterpillars, and praying mantises. Place each kind of insect in a separate container. A suitable container may be made from a milk carton or plastic detergent bottle, thoroughly washed. Cut openings in the containers. Place a twig or small branch in the container to give the insect something to climb on. Tape pieces of sheer nylon hose or screen over the openings. Feed the insects leaves from the plant on which they were found. Use a magnifying glass to observe the insects. After observing them for a few hours, return them to their natural outdoor home. If kept in this container they would die, and we don't want that to happen.

Socrates used to say that if he could get up to the highest place in Athens, he would lift up his voice and proclaim, "What mean ye, fellow-citizens, that ye turn every stone to scrape wealth together, and take so little care of your children, to whom, one day, ye must relinquish it all?"

83

ANT FARMS. Make the ant farm container from a transparent plastic box with a tightly fitting lid. Fill the box three-quarters full with loose sand. Punch several small holes in the lid of the box with the tip of a heated ice pick. Plug the holes with cotton to prevent the ants from escaping. Air will pass through the cotton. Add the ants which you have found in your yard. Place the lid on securely and tape it closed.

All men are like grass, and all their glory is like the flowers of the field; the grass withers and the flowers fall, but the word of the Lord stands forever.
—1 Peter 1:24-25

Feed the ants by dropping syrup from a medicine dropper through the holes in the lid. Add a few drops of water to the soil to provide moisture. Feed the ants twice a week.

Handle the box gently so the ant tunnels are not disturbed. The ants will be more active if the sides of the box are covered with paper towels or newspaper except when observing the ants.

AN INEXPENSIVE terrarium is a fun project. Place a layer of gravel on the bottom of a large glass bowl for drainage. Cover the gravel with potting soil or use two parts of regular soil, two parts of sand, and one part of peat moss.

Make tiny holes in the soil for the roots of small plants or plant cuttings, and set the plants gently but firmly in the soil. Level the soil, then water lightly. Cover the terrarium with plastic wrap and place it where it will receive daylight but not direct sun. The terrarium should be watered once a month. Observe how moisture condenses on the sides of the bowl and then returns to the soil. If the glass clouds up too much, slide the covering plastic wrap to one side for a few hours to permit fresh air to enter the bowl.

USE PLASTIC medicine droppers to avoid messy spills when watering plants. Place a small amount of water in a shallow unbreakable pan. Fill the dropper and give the plants a drink. This works well for very young children.

GRASS GROWING. Soak a pinecone overnight in water. Sprinkle it liberally with grass seed. Stand the cone in a shallow container of water. Place the container near a window so there is light for the grass to grow. As the grass grows, trim it with scissors so that it looks like a miniature tree.

The next time you serve corn-on-the-cob, save the cob. Sprinkle it with grass seed and carefully set it in a pan of water. Place the pan near a window. As the grass grows it becomes a floating garden.

MAKE FLOATING candles by melting wax into empty English walnut shells. Place string in them for wicks. Add chips of crayon to the melting wax for coloring. Be sure to melt the wax in a double boiler or over very low heat, watching it continually.

FAST-GROWING GARDEN. Prepare a shallow pan with loose dirt. Dig little holes and drop in birdseed. Cover the seeds with a thin layer of dirt and water generously. Keep the seeds in a warm place with lots of light and they should begin to sprout in just a few days. They will need watering about every three days.

STAR LIGHT, STAR BRIGHT. Bring the twinkling night sky into your room. Begin by choosing a picture of a night sky or single constellation from an encyclopedia or astronomy book. Use this picture as a pattern to make a similar picture on a piece of construction paper. For each star in the picture, use a needle to poke a corresponding hole in the construction paper. Hold a flashlight up to the paper while in a darkened room and the stars will shine on the ceiling.

Building boys and girls is better than mending men and women.

To be loved, be lovable.

WEATHER WATCHERS. Begin charting the changes in the weather as a project. Start recording the daily high and low temperatures (in Fahrenheit and centigrade), wind speed and direction, wind description (calm, slight breeze, strong, etc.), wind effect (smoke goes straight up, weather vanes turn, flags flutter, trees sway, etc.), precipitation amounts, barometer readings, etc. At the end of a week or month, determine the average temperature, amount of rainfall, etc. Make a graph of the monthly findings to compare the overall year's weather.

DIVING APPLE SEEDS. With carbon dioxide, you can make apple seeds dive down and come up again in a glass of water. Put a level teaspoonful of baking soda into a dry glass. Put three teaspoons of vinegar into another glass half filled with water. Add several apple seeds to the soda glas. Now pour the vinegar and water mixture into the soda glass. Watch the fizz as the gas forms. What happens to the seeds? They move! They dance! They will dive and rise again for quite some time. What makes the seeds dive and dance? The gas bubbles attach themselves to the seeds and the seeds rise and fall with the bubbles.

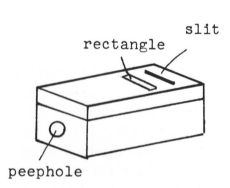

STAR-STUDDED PEEP BOX SHOW. You can gaze at the stars in the comfort of your room ... all you need is a shoe box, some small paper stars, construction paper, and these directions. At one end of the shoe box cut a hole about the size of a half-dollar to serve as a peephole. At the opposite end of the lid, cut out a rectangle to allow light to enter. Behind this opening, cut a slit slightly wider than five inches.

To make a star card you will need a 3 by 5 inch piece of blue construction paper, a black felt pen, and some silver stars. Using a diagram in an encyclopedia or book on stars as a guide, draw the major constellations . . . one to a card, marking the locations of the stars. Paste the silver stars in the correct places and make a tiny hole in the center of each with a pin point. Holding the card horizontally, write the name of the constellation along the top.

Slide the card through the slit in the lid. As you look through the peephole the light will shine through illuminating the stars and outlining the constellation.

MINIATURE GREENHOUSE. Children love planting seeds and watching them grow. The activity can be even more fun when they make their own greenhouse from a large cardboard box and clear plastic wrap. Rectangle boxes about 20 by 8 by 8 inches work best. Cut out the four sides of the box leaving about ½ inch at each edge. Cover the frame with plastic wrap secured with masking tape. Make a lid by cutting a hole in the top and covering it with a plastic flap using tape around the edge to provide an airtight seal. The greenhouse works well for growing pole beans. Plant the seeds in plastic cups filled with garden soil and sand, mixed in equal amounts. Water the soil well. No more watering should be needed. Place the greenhouse in light but not in direct sun.

MARBLE MAGNIFYING GLASS. With the help of a marble you will be able to see many things in more detail than with the naked eye. You will need a clear glass marble or one that has very little color. A clear plastic bead sometimes works well. You will also need plenty of light with your marble magnifier. Hold the marble near—almost touching—the object to be viewed and put your eye almost as close to the opposite side of the marble. By moving the marble very slightly nearer to or farther from the object, you will find a line of sight that brings into focus and greatly magnifies a very small area.

Whatever you do, work at it with all your heart, as working for the Lord, not for men, since you know that you will receive an inheritance from the Lord as a reward. It is the Lord Christ you are serving.
—Colossians 4:11

POCKET MICROSCOPE. Cut a short length of cardboard tube from a roll of paper towels. Fit a piece of plastic wrap firmly over one end of the tube and secure it in place with a rubber band. Hold the tube vertical, with the plastic-wrapped end down. The pocket scope does not use enough water to cause the plastic to sag, so the sag has to be made before any water is poured in. This is so you will be able to keep a drop of water in the middle of the scope. To do this, put a pencil, eraser end down, into the opening end of the tube and press it against the center of the plastic to form a slight cup. Then put a couple drops of water into the cup. Hold the wrapped end (the lens end) close to the object you want to magnify and put your eye right down to the open end of the tube. As you look through the drops of water, things will be magnified.

Ninety percent of the friction of daily life is caused by the tone of voice.
—Arnold Bennett

MAGNETIC FISHING GAME. Tie a magnet to a piece of string. Tie the other end of the string to a wooden dowel or stick. Cut out fish shapes from paper and put a letter of the alphabet on each one. Fasten a paper clip to each fish. Put the fish in a box and "go fishing." As the fish are caught, the child says the letter or number on the fish. If he gives the wrong answer, that fish goes back into the box.

WATER PLAY. Fill a large basin or the bathtub with water—not too cold and not too warm, but comfortable to the touch. Provide the following accessories for your child to use: funnel, eyedropper, plastic clothes sprinkler, plastic measuring cup, sponge, tea strainer, plastic squeeze bottles, measuring spoons, and some corks for boats. The child will have a great time experimenting with the various utensils as he measures, sorts, pours, and observes the movement of water. Be sure both the child and the area are "dressed" for the occasion.

PAPERMAKING. Collect an old newspaper, a mixing bowl, an eggbeater, a wood block, a square of window screen (3 to 4 inches square), a plastic sandwich bag, wallpaper paste or corn starch, water, and a tablespoon.

Fill the bowl one fourth full of water. Tear one-half of the newspaper page into pieces. Place the pieces in the bowl and soak them for an hour. After the paper has become thoroughly soaked, beat it with the eggbeater. This will break the paper into fibers. When the mixture has been thoroughly beaten, it should be creamy like wood pulp.

Dissolve two heaping tablespoons of wallpaper paste or corn starch in a pint of water. Pour into the pulp and stir. Hold the piece of window screen flat and lower it into the pulp. Repeat this step until you accumulate a layer of pulp about one tenth of an inch thick. Set the pulp-covered screen on a newspaper and place a plastic bag over it. Press down with the wood block, gently, then with more pressure. The water will filter through the screen onto the newspaper. Allow the fibers to dry for about 24 hours. Peel the fiber from the screen and you will have a piece of recycled paper.

Summer is the season when children slam the doors they left open all winter.

CLOUD PICTURES. Gaze out the window at the fluffy white clouds. What shape can you see? There may be animals, nursery rhyme characters, and other shapes.

MAGNETS come in different shapes, but they all will attract only objects made of iron or steel. Compare horseshoe magnets, U-shaped magnets, bar magnets, and cylindrical magnets. Collect a variety of items and see which ones can be picked up by a magnet.

Place a magnet in a drinking glass. Tie a string to a paper clip and hold it near the glass. The magnet will pull the paper clip toward the glass.

It isn't your position that makes you happy or unhappy. It's your disposition.

SECRET WRITING. You can send secret messages to your friends by writing to them with ink that no one can see! Write your secrets with a pen dipped in lemon juice. Your friends will hold the paper over a light bulb to see the writing. The heat will make the lemon juice turn brown so that the message can be read.

MAGNIFIED SALT. Shake a few grains of salt onto the table. Look at it through a magnifying glass. The lens will show you that each grain is really a shiny little block. What does sugar look like?

SHADOW CLOCK. On a bright sunny day push a pencil half way through a paper plate. Poke the pencil in the ground. The pencil will make a shadow on the plate. Make a mark where the shadow falls. Leave it alone for an hour. When you come back, where is the shadow? The sun has moved, time has passed. People in biblical times used clocks like this—clocks that told time by the placement of shadows.

A pattern for a paper plate sundial appears in chapter 10.

PAPER CUP STETHOSCOPE. Cut the bottom out of a paper cup. Put the big end on a friend's chest right over his heart. Press your ear against the cup. Do not touch the cup with your hands, but listen very quietly. You will hear his heart beating . . . THUMP! THUMP!

After you have finished with the stethoscope, turn your cup into a HUMMER. Attach a piece of waxed paper to the large end with a rubber band. Touch your lips to the waxed paper and hum into it. The humming makes the air move, and the air makes the waxed paper move, and the cup hums right along with you.

TUBE BINOCULARS. Paint and decorate two toilet tissue cardboard rolls. Glue them together side by side and attach a string or piece of yarn for a neck strap. You have now created a pair of binoculars. Look out the window at the trees, birds, and clouds.

A luxury is anything you don't need that you can't do without.

LEARNING IS CHILD'S PLAY... OR SO THEY SAY

CHAPTER 7

Fathers, do not exasperate your children; instead, bring them up in the training and instruction of the Lord.
—Ephesians 6:4

When do humans make their debut into society? When they are born into the common life of the family. A family is a society, and it is an educational institution of the first significance. Through their parents children are under the tutelage of the traditions, customs, and economic conditions that have made the parents what they are. In the intimacy of the family every member, young or old, is a feeling part of social processes. Children are included within a network of concrete relations between persons.

Family life is famishing for want of deep acquaintance between parents and their own offspring. When a parent and child frolic together they become acquainted with each other. Each finds in the other personality riches that would otherwise, perhaps, be unsuspected. And not only do common pleasures reveal one to another, but they help toward the deep and permanent attachments that hold through adversity as well as through happiness. Thus it is that playing together, enjoying literature, music, and pictures together, making family excursions together, and even common indulgence in jolly nonsense have the deep ethical value of

92

joining person to person in a society of reciprocal good will and love.

The fireside is a seminary of infinite importance. Few can receive the honors of a college but all are graduates of the home. The learning of the university may fade from the recollection, its classic lore may grow faint in the halls of memory; but the simple lessons of home, enameled upon the heart of childhood, defy the rust of years and outlive the more mature but less vivid pictures of later years.

Many processes are used by adults in solving both simple and complex problems. These are processes of decision making. And these are the same processes that young children need to learn to come to grips with their world—observing, inferring, classifying, and communicating.

Observing: using the five senses (seeing, smelling, touching, tasting, hearing) to examine things.

Inferring: using previous experiences to discover additional information about something.

Classifying: grouping or sorting things according to descriptive characteristics, such as size, shape, color.

Communicating: the ability to tell what was learned through the other three processes.

Learning to use these processes promotes intellectual growth, provides potential for greater success in school, and helps develop a more positive self-image. Children gain more interest and curiosity about the world around them. And because they do a good deal of individual exploring with different materials, they soon begin to realize there is more than one approach to a problem and often more than one solution. Most important is the fact that children learn that they can be successful in doing things for and by themselves.

Nobody ever added up the value of a smile;
We know how much a dollar's worth and how much is a mile;
We know the distance to the sun, the size and weight of earth —
But no one's ever told us yet how much a smile is worth.

Learning is a process which engages the hearts and bodies of children as well as their minds. We set the stage for such learning with equipment and atmosphere that we provide. Children learn eagerly when they are stimulated through experiences which are interesting to them and when they are able to reinforce knowledge they have gained through play activities.

Following is a listing of skills and learning objectives that can be nurtured in the home:

Motor skills

recognition of body parts
balancing
walking
running
jumping
hopping
skipping
throwing
catching
climbing

Hand-eye coordination

cutting
tracing
copying shapes
puzzle/maze solution
letter, number, symbol reproduction from memory
pasting
duplicating patterns
reproducing designs

Manual dexterity:

lacing   braiding
sewing   arranging
stringing   stenciling

Visual comprehension

colors
letters/numbers
concepts such as top, middle, bottom, front, back, inside, outside
shapes
size differences
name recognition
letter matching
recognition of common labels and symbols
recognition of visual similarities
recognition of visual differences
picture interpretation
word construction and printing

Auditory comprehension

recognition of ordinal concepts such as first, second, third, etc.
use of complete sentences
ability to answer questions with use of thought
lengthening of attention span/ listening development
memorization development
story recall and retelling (including plot, main ideas, characters)
word definition
understanding opposites
vocabulary development
development of proper grammar usage
recognition of environmental sounds
recognition of sound similarities and differences
recognition of beginning word sounds, middle word sounds, ending word sounds
word rhyming
creative expression

Mathematical concepts awareness

one-to-one counting
geometric shapes
reading and writing numbers
counting and recognition of sets
size words such as big/little, long/longer/longest, tall/short
finding parts of things (beginning fractions)
measuring, beginning metrics, length, weight, distance
beginning money concepts
time concepts:
    calendars (days, weeks, months, years)
    clocks (seconds, minutes, hours), seasons
counting by 2s, by 5s, and by 10s
beginning addition and subtraction

Social studies

family relationships
community relationships and awareness
world awareness (other peoples/nationalities)
national history
manners, social graces, self-discipline, responsibility
biographies
patriotic awareness and responsibility

Nature and science conceptual awareness

living things (animals, insects, plants)
earth and sky
beginning geography
water and air
microscopic observations
machines, magnets, electricity
the human body and how it works:
    the senses
    posture
    safety
    health care
    diet, nutrition
    first aid

Music and drama

scale recognition
voice control
rhythmic movement
puppetry
rhythmic expression and rhythm band
timing and musical patterns
instrumental investigation and awareness
sound and tone variation
types of music (modern, classical, folk, etc.)
story dramatization
records (stories, songs, rhymes)
cassette recording for voice and speech awareness
speech refinement
choral speaking

Physical education

exercises
games
obstacle courses
races
indoor and outdoor large and small muscle activities

Religious awareness

God, the Creator
Jesus, the Son
understanding of terms such as "sin," "gospel," and "salvation"
Bible stories
Christian songs, rhymes, etc.
celebration of Christian festivals (Christmas, Easter, etc.)

Arts and crafts

a variety of projects and procedures involving the senses and inspiring individual creativity

USE descriptive words to help expand your child's vocabulary. Some samples are: dry, dusty, light, heavy, crumbly, squishy, hard, soft, wet, dark, damp, cool, gritty—and don't be afraid to use "scientific" terms.

Children have more need of models than critics.

GIVE your child a piece of paper and have him (or her) follow directions such as, write "A" at the top of the page, draw a circle in the middle of the page, place an "X" in the bottom right-hand corner of the page. This helps teach parts of a page as well as giving practice in following directions, both of which are necessary in reading readiness.

RELATE reading to the child's world by encouraging the child to read cereal boxes, candy wrappers, can and jar labels.

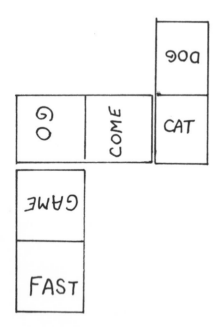

USE large index cards to make a set of word dominoes. Write two words on the face of each card with a line drawn between. The words on any domino should not begin with the same sound. To play, the child takes a domino from the pile and reads it aloud. If a word on the domino has the same beginning sound as the domino on the table, the child places it next to that one, lining up the matching word sounds. Play continues until the child is unable to make a match.

USE Bible-related words and pictures to help children use their reading skills to learn of Bible-times people and objects. On 9 by 12 inch pieces of paper, draw each alphabet letter with a felt pen. Use capital letters. Beside each letter, glue or tape a Bible-related picture, the name of which begins with that letter. Use them as flash cards or for games.

STRING is a useful teaching tool. Give your children a 36-inch length of string or yarn and have them follow these directions: make a circle on the floor with the string; stand inside the circle; jump out of the circle; put two feet in the circle; make the circle into a triangle, a square, a straight line.

BUILDING blocks and a sheet of cardboard provide a medium for learning activities. Cut a large cardboard square and put it on the floor. Give the child six building blocks and have him or her follow these directions: make two stacks of blocks, one stack with two blocks and one stack with three blocks; put one block in each corner of the board; put five blocks in a row; make six blocks into two rows; build a tall stack and a short stack.

Adult education is when parents help their children with their home-work.

COLLECT sound words and draw pictures of the sound being made, such as: squeak, pop, creak, boom, crash, sneeze, snore, snap, scratch, ring, and snap.

LARGE wall toys with moving parts are easy to make and fun for young chidren to manipulate. Cut the toys from heavy cardboard. For example, cut out the body and head of an elephant. Cut separate pieces for fat legs, a tail, and large ears. Fasten these pieces onto the body with paper fasteners. The legs, ears, and tail should move easily. Hang the animal on a wall within easy reach of the child.

USE a square napkin or piece of paper. Draw lines where it is to be folded. Lay the paper on a table and let your child practice folding it on the lines. This develops muscular control of the fingers which is training for precision.

When a task is once
* begun,*
Never leave it till it's done.
Be the labor great or
* small,*
Do it well or not at all.

MAKE up an animal! Fill a box with scraps of paper, each with a single letter of the alphabet written on it. Have the children pick out four or five letters and assemble them any way they want to make the name of a brand-new animal. Have them describe the animal—where it lives, what it eats, etc. Have them demonstrate the way the animal moves, the way it sleeps, the way it plays, the way it communicates.

HAND MUSCLES can be developed by using the following procedures. Give a sheet of newspaper to the child and see how much of it he (or she) can crumple with just one hand holding the paper in the air (you may have to start with a quarter of a sheet and gradually increase the size). Draw a small circle on a piece of paper and let the child use a crayon to make larger and larger circles around it. Draw a simple maze for the child to follow with his finger and then with a crayon, staying within the path.

PROVIDE the child with a pencil and piece of paper. Then let her proceed to take an inventory of things in the room. Count everything. How many chairs? Tables? Books? Pictures? Doors? Write down the listing or draw pictures of the main categories and put the number found next to the drawing.

CHILDREN need help in learning their numbers. Make it fun. Ask them to count in a way that they play and learn at the same time. For example: Can you jump up and down three times? Can you hop on one foot two times? Can you wiggle your finger five times? Also play the game this way: How many times can you jump up and down? Show me. Let me hear you count the times.

Without faith we are like stained-glass windows in the dark.

TO HELP your child learn the days of the week, set up a bulletin board with spaces for each of the days of the week. At the end of each day, put up a note or a picture that shows something special that happened that day. At the end of the week, discuss the special thing that happened each day. Also look ahead by trying to determine if some of the same things might take place the next week.

TURN discarded calendar pages into number and word cards. Cut the various parts: the date, day, and month. Mount them on separate pieces of lightweight cardboard to make flash cards.

MAKE a paper loop chain containing as many loops as there are days in the current month. Use one color for the week days, another color for Saturdays and Sundays, and a special color for special days, such as Christmas or the Fourth of July. Use another color to indicate the child's birthday. At the start of each day, remove the previous day's loop. Put the discarded loops into another chain to keep track of past time.

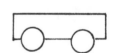

TURN geometric shapes into pictures. Cut various shapes (squares, circles, triangles, rectangles) from construction paper. Arrange them to make pictures.

REMOVE the top from an egg carton and number the sections from one to twelve. Collect 78 small objects, such as beans, and store them in a covered pan. Let the child fill each cup with the correct number of "eggs," putting one bean in the cup marked "1," two beans in the cup marked "2," etc.

You will never "find" time to do anything. If you want time, you must take it.

CHILDREN begin to develop an interest in puzzles at an early age. To make a sturdy puzzle you will need one piece of Masonite or ¼ inch plywood about 9 by 12 inches in size, one colorful picture, white glue, clear plastic spray, fine sandpaper, and a felt pen. Brush the glue on the Masonite. Lay the picture on the glue-covered board and smooth out the wrinkles. Let it dry. Spray the picture with clear plastic and let that dry. Mark the picture with a puzzle pattern, taking care to keep it simple and not to mark through faces. Cut the puzzle pieces with a jigsaw and label each piece of the puzzle on the back with a felt pen. Sand the edges of the puzzle pieces to assure smoothness. Store the puzzle in a box or large envelope labeled with the same code you used in marking the back of the puzzle pieces.

ON a table (or floor) place eight Styrofoam cups, about six inches apart, in a row. The child stacks the cups large end to large end, small end to small end, until they are either all in the stack or tumble down. This is a good coordination game.

INSTRUCTION in the use of scissors can result in greatly improved cutting skills. A valuable hint, useful in cutting a small item from a large piece of paper, is to cut the small item from the large paper crudely. The child can then more easily handle the item, having a less bulky area with which to cope. It's also helpful to point out that it helps to turn the paper containing the item to be cut. Draw some lines (jagged, curvy, straight, circular) for the child to practice cutting.

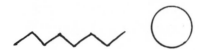

EGG cartons are useful for teaching fractions. Cut off the tops from five egg cartons. Now, leave one bottom section whole, cut one in half crosswise leaving six cups in each half, cut one in thirds with four cups in each section, cut one in fourths with three cups in each section, and cut one in sixths leaving two cups in each section. How many fourths does it take to make a whole? How many thirds does it take to hold as many eggs as the whole? The child can place the sections together to answer such questions.

MAKE shape booklets by cutting the cover and pages in the shape of a circle, a rectangle, a triangle, etc. The child searches magazines for pictures of objects which match those shapes, cuts them out, and pastes them into the appropriate books.

ONE-TO-ONE concept. Put five objects on a table. Touch each object as you count them—one, two, three, four, five. Now have your child touch and count the objects. Watch to see that he or she does not touch the same object while counting one, two. Practice until he grasps the idea of one count for one object. Take the child's hand and move it from object to object as you count together. For a variation, clap your hands and count each time, or march around the room and count as you take each step.

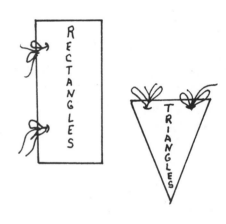

MAKE 4 by 6 inch posterboard cards. Print a capital letter on one card and the small letter on another card. Make a set for each letter of the alphabet. Paste or draw a picture of something starting with each letter on other cards. Punch a hole at the top of each card. Mix all the cards together in a box. Provide several shoestrings or pieces of yarn with a knot at one end. The child finds and laces up the three cards that belong together for each letter—capital, small letter, picture.

101

CUT colored cartoons (or find pictures of well-known stories). Place these in a box or spread them out on the floor or table. Have the child place the pictures in proper sequence and orally tell the story.

HAVE your child help you dip five-inch pieces of string in liquid starch. As you remove the string, lightly squeeze out the excess starch. Shape the piece of string to form the capital and small letters on separate cardboard squares. After the starched letters dry, the child can paint them with tempera paint. These now become raised letters on the squares which the child can trace with a finger to become acquainted with the form of each letter. Add to the tactile experience by having the child identify the letters while blindfolded.

The toughest problem some children face is that of learning good manners without seeing any.

PRACTICE beginning word sounds by playing a game called "I see." Take turns saying, "I see something in the room that begins with the sound 'S.'" (Say the sound, not the letter name.) After the item is guessed, the other person gets to choose an item in the room beginning with another letter sound.

PREPARE drawings of strung beads arranged in various color patterns. Have your child choose a picture and duplicate the pattern by stringing beads to match the color combinations.

RULE a large sheet of paper into 28 rectangle sections (seven columns down and four across). Write a capital letter in each section, but not in alphabetical order. In the two extra spaces write "Garage." Use 26 small car shapes as playing pieces. Write a small letter on each car. Park the cars in the "Garage" spaces. The child picks a car and "parks" it in the matching letter space.

GIVE your child several wooden pegs and two small cardboard circles. The child can use these items to construct pictures by putting the pegs and circles together.

OBTAIN paint color sample squares from a paint store. Get various colors and shades. Mix up the colors and let your child arrange them in order of gradation, going from darkest to lightest for each color.

CUT cardboard tubes into various lengths and have your child arrange them so they form a pattern of increasing lengths.

COLLECT buttons, keys, and/or thread spools of various sizes and shapes. The more you collect the better. Your child will spend a lot of time sorting these items according to size, shape, and color.

A SIMPLE ring toss game can be made from a shallow cardboard box, five rubber jar rings, and 10 clothespins. Cut 10 holes in the underside of the box. Number the holes and then stick a clothespin in each hole. Toss the rubber rings over the clothespins and call out the number you have circled.

103

MAKE your own chalkboard. Use a piece of plywood or heavy cardboard of whatever size you want. You can purchase chalkboard paint at your paint store or make your own. Mix one pint of quick-drying enamel (any color) with plaster of paris. Wet the plaster with paint thinner until you make a paste, using about ½ as much plaster as you have enamel. Mix the plaster into the enamel until smooth. Paint it onto the board and let it dry thoroughly. Give it a second coat and let that dry. You now have a nice, inexpensive chalkboard.

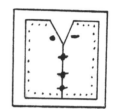

TO HELP your children learn how to tie, zip, button, and snap, construct some manipulative items for them to practice with. Attach a piece of material to a wooden frame. The material pieces should have a zipper, buttons and buttonholes, snaps and ribbons. The frame holds the material firm while the children work with them.

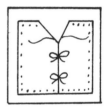

MAKE a picture the shape of a telephone (front view) and mount it on a piece of cardboard. To make the dial, cut out 10 holes around the edge of a large circle. Attach the dial to the telephone with a paper fastener. Write the numbers of the dial through the openings. Your child can practice dialing your own telephone number. Have the child write your number at the bottom of the telephone picture, or in the center of the dial.

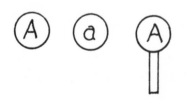

INSTEAD of making alphabet flash cards for learning letter names, make letter lollipops. Cut two circles for each letter. Use different colors of construction paper for the different letters. On one circle print the capital letter; on the other circle print the small letter. Cut a rectangular piece of cardboard for each set of letters. Now insert the cardboard between two circles and paste these all together to make a lollipop letter.

KEEP some graph paper on hand, or make your own by drawing small squares on sheets of paper. The child begins this game by writing a word in the upper left corner. Then she thinks of a word beginning with the last letter of that word. She writes it, going down the paper from the last letter of the first word. She continues in this way until she reaches the bottom of the paper. She can then turn the paper upside down and start all over again.

T	O	P											
		E											
		T	O	E									
				E									
			L	I	D								
					A								
					R								
					K	I	N	G					
								O					
								L					
								F	U	N	N	Y	

PLACE a milk carton against a wall with the open side facing out. Have your child roll a ball from across the room into the milk carton. This is a good game for hand-eye coordination.

STAND up straight and drop pebbles (or some other small objects) into a paper cup. How many went in?

CIRCLE all the D's (or other letter or word) you can find on one page of the newspaper. Wait until your father has finished reading it!

Billy was in a store with his mother when he was given a stick of candy by one of the clerks.
"What do you say, Billy?" said his mother.
"Charge it!" he replied.

105

CLOSE your eyes and listen. Shhhhh! How many different sounds can you hear? What are they?

WEIGHING can be fun by using a pie plate balance scale. You will need two aluminum pie plates, one coat hanger, some wire or string. Punch holes in the edges of the pie plates and tie wire or string through them. Tie the other end (about 8 inches in length) to the ends of the coat hanger. Hang the coat hanger from a string in a doorway. Your child can find objects to weigh, determining which objects weigh more, less, or the same.

If you wish to bring up a child in the way he should go, be sure you are going that way yourself.

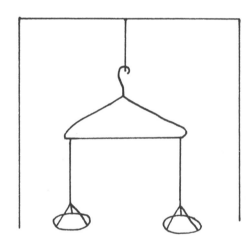

LEARN how to dial the "Operator" in the event of an emergency. The telephone company will help you with suggestions in teaching your child this important procedure.

MAKE a long list of vegetables, animals, machines, etc. Put them in alphabetical order. How many of them can you illustrate with pictures?

FIND your family name in the telephone book. How many others are there with the same name?

TRACE around items of different sizes or shapes, such as blocks, cookie cutters, lids, etc., to create designs on a sheet of paper. This is a great aid in developing small-muscle control.

OBTAIN a carpet sample or cover a piece of heavy cardboard with a fabric which has a nap, such as upholstery or drapery material or felt. Provide several pieces of yarn, different colors and lengths. Your child can "draw" pictures on the fabric or carpeting by arranging the pieces of yarn. The yarn will cling to the fabric when it is held up.

USE an old cookie sheet for a magnetic board. Cut out pictures, letters, numbers, etc., and glue a small piece of magnet to the back of each. Self-sticking strip magnet can be purchased at craft or office supply stores. It is inexpensive and can be cut to the desired size.

Happiness is a homemade article.
—English proverb

MAKE a see-through board. Use a piece of heavy cardboard or plywood about 9 by 12 inches in size. Cover this with a piece of clear plastic. Overlap the plastic on two ends of the board and glue it to the back. Leave the top and bottom open. You can insert pictures or printed words behind the clear plastic. Your child can trace them through the plastic with a crayon or washable felt pen. The plastic can be wiped off and used again and again.

WRITE numbers or letters around the top of a shoe box. Write corresponding numbers and letters on spring-type clothespins. Your child can fasten the clothespins around the top of the box to match the ones written on the box.

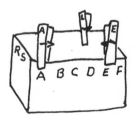

HERE is an exciting board to use for learning games. Half-inch plywood works well for this. Cut two pieces, 2 by 3 feet each. Hinge them in the middle so they can be folded. Drill 15 holes on each board and insert a bolt and nut. Attach insulated bell wire to the 15 bolts on one board.

After all the bolts are inserted, with bell wire attached, connect the wires. Give each side a number, then wire in scrambled order, such as number 1 of left side to number 5 of right side until all the wires are connected.

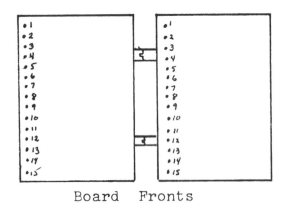

Board   Fronts

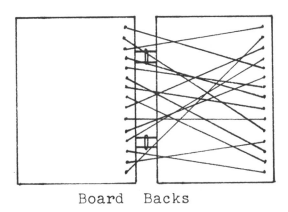

Board   Backs

Strips of grooved wood nailed to the front of the board will hold your word strip questions (on left) and answers (on right).

The most expensive part of this project will be to purchase a fire alarm bell, 6-volt battery, and two long lead wires. Attach one end of the wire to the bell and from the bell to the other lead.

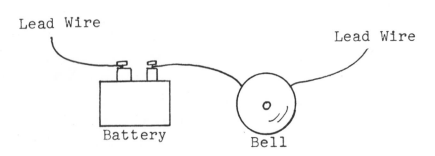

Lead Wire

Lead Wire

Battery

Bell

Compile a list of 15 questions. Write them on pieces of posterboard and lay on strips of grooved wood. Write the answers on separate pieces of posterboard. These must be placed in their correct positions on the opposite board.

Your child can match the answers with the questions. Contacts are made on the quiz board by holding the lead wires in each hand and touching the metal bolt beside each question and corresponding answer. When a contact is made, the bell will ring.

CUT the shape of a person, about ½ life-size, from felt or flannel. Attach this to a wall. Next, cut out items of clothing (shirt, pants, socks, shoes, and hair, eyes, lips, etc.) also from felt or flannel. Your child will have a good time "dressing" the person. You might cut out different clothing for changes in the weather, such as boots, raincoats, hats, mittens, shorts, swimming suits, umbrellas, etc. Also cut different colors for hair and eyes, and differently shaped lips to indicate smiles and frowns.

DRAW the outline of a simple object on a piece of cardboard with a felt pen. Punch holes along the outline. Provide a piece of yarn or a long shoestring and let your child lace around the picture. If you use yarn dip one end of it in white glue and let it dry to give it a stiffness for lacing through the holes. There are some patterns you can use for this in chapter 10.

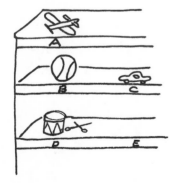

DOES your child keep putting things away in the wrong places? Give shelves a code. Put a different letter on each shelf and put the same letter on the boxes, toys, etc., that belong on that shelf. When through with an item, have your child look for the "magic letter" that matches the item with the shelf where it belongs. The items and shelves could be color coded for children who can not read yet.

109

QUIET TIMES AND SHARING TIMES

CHAPTER 8

For the Lord God is a sun and shield; the Lord bestows favor and honor; no good thing does he withhold from those whose walk is blameless.
—Psalm 84:11

The family is the most potent influence in the development of personality. It may be the most effective means of education. The family wants more than anything else to make sure that each child gets the most out of life. The nature and function of the family give it distinct advantages in education. It has the growing child first, and for the largest amount of time during the years of greatest responsiveness. It brings to bear on the child the education which comes from social participation and fellowship. The family is in the most favorable position to make use of the child's current interests and needs. It provides a constant living example of what it seeks to teach in Christian living.

A family is a giving, sharing, loving institution. It gives gifts, but not in the way we most often think of gifts. A gift is more than a physical object or gesture. It is personal communication. It has about it the aura of friendship from the giver and the additional charm of the joy of the receiver. For all of us gifts can be a portion of ourselves if, in giving, we think first of the one to whom we give; if, in receiving, we think first of the giver.

In a family situation each member of the

family will contribute personal service which is a thing that money cannot buy and that cannot be done by proxy. Doing for oneself all that one is competent to do is a significant contribution to the family and is highly educative. Self-reliant experimentation must be encouraged even though we are certain that errors will be made. Children should not be shielded too much from the uncomfortable effects of their errors. The important thing is not to get the most perfect possible immediate result, but to promote growth, to develop individuality that is both independent and cooperative.

Books can help young children understand themselves and their relationships to other people. Books can help prepare them for future experiences, both pleasant and unpleasant. Books can nourish the interests of children and their enjoyment of words and their sounds and meanings. Encourage your children to get into books, to learn from books, to gain experience from books.

Even before they hear Bible stories, and long before they hear any discussion of the nature and teachings of the Bible, little children can begin to sense the special significance of this book. They can know that this book has special meaning, and that it is of special value to their parents. Before they receive any definite teaching about the Bible, they may develop an attitude of expectancy toward it.

It should be this way for most books, for they contain messages that relate personally to each reader. These messages help develop the person's ideas and ideals. They help develop a person who is able to go forth and share interests, knowledge, and life with others.

For us to help children find themselves and achieve success, we must ourselves keep growing and feel good about ourselves. Our good feelings can help our children develop healthy personalities. And such children can make the world a better place in which to live.

If everyone swept in front of his own house, the whole world would be clean.

111

DISCUSS with children the proper way to handle books. This might include:

1. Our hands are clean.
2. We turn pages by the upper right hand corner.
3. We turn pages carefully so we don't rip or wrinkle the pages.
4. We never draw or write in books—unless it is a workbook or coloring book.
5. We use flat paper bookmarks (a bulky or fat object breaks the book's back).
6. We never lay a book upside down with pages open (this also breaks its back).
7. We never leave books lying around on the floor to be stepped on or get dirty.

Books are precious and should be cared for properly.

A poor appetite for books may lead to intellectual malnutrition.

"OLD MOTHER GOOSE" was a real person whose maiden name was Foster. Born near Charlestown, Massachusetts, in 1665, she married Isaac Goose, who died years later, leaving her a widow with ten children. For the entertainment of her large brood, she wrote a great number of nursery rhymes which were collected and published by her son-in-law, Thomas Fleet. When Old Mother Goose died at the age of 92, she was buried in Old Granary Cemetery, Boston, where her grave may still be seen.

LINE VIEWER. Cut a piece of cardboard about half the size of the page of a child's book. Cut a rectangular hole in the cardboard large enough to frame one line of print. This viewer helps the child who is learning to read and who may still have difficulty following the printed lines. Place the viewer on the page, moving it from one line to the next as the child reads.

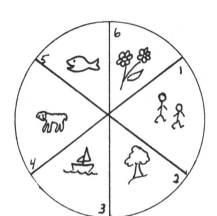

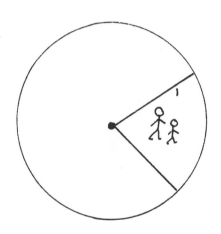

RECORDED READING. Use the tape or cassette recorder to help with reading. Have children tape themselves reading aloud. Then have them play back the reading to hear their performance. This often brings about increased awareness of reading faults or problems and helps children improve their reading ability.

STORY WHEEL. Cut two round discs, 12 inches in diameter, from posterboard or other thin cardboard. Draw lines on each disc to divide the circle into six equal pie-shaped sections. Cut one of the sections from one of the discs. Draw or paste pictures illustrating a story on the other disc. Arrange the pictures in order of sequence, numbering the sections from one to six. Put the disc with the missing section on top of the picture disc and fasten the two together in the center with a paper fastener. As you or your child rotates the top disc, the one with the missing section, the story pictures will show through the opening. You can tell the story, scene by scene, as you turn the wheel. Pictures for additional stories can be prepared on separate paper discs to be inserted between the two cardboard discs.

STORY BOARD. You will need a piece of Styrofoam about 9 by 12 inches in size, about 1 inch thick. Cut slits lengthwise in the Styrofoam about ½ inch deep and about 1 to 2 inches apart. Cut pictures of people, animals, etc., from magazines. Paste a piece of cardboard to the back of each for strength. The pictures can be inserted in the slits in the Styrofoam to make them stand. As you or your child tells a story, keep adding pictures until the scene is completed.

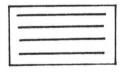

Little Judy concluded her prayer by saying: "Dear God, before I finish, please take care of daddy, take care of mommy, take care of my baby brother, grandma, and grandpa . . . and please, God, take care of yourself, or else we're all sunk!"

CLEANUP. Everyone needs to be involved in the chores involved with keeping up a home. Have your child look for pictures or draw jobs that need to be done around the house: dusting, sweeping, window washing, picking up things, washing and drying dishes, etc. He might prepare a chart to keep track of the jobs he wants to do in coming days or weeks to help. Put a picture of the job under the name of the day he wants to do it. When the job is completed on that day, draw a big red star over the picture.

BEAT THE BELL. To help your child pick up her toys and other things around the house, use a timer with a bell. Start the timer and have her see how much she can get picked up and put away before the bell rings. It may take several rounds with the timer before everything gets picked up, but it's better than nagging!

GAMES, PUZZLES, RIDDLES, TONGUE TWISTERS, FINGER PLAYS, POEMS, QUIZZES, AND JOKES are fun and provide hours of entertainment for children. Following are some of these various activities. After your children have tried these, perhaps they can make up some original ones to share with each other.

WOULDN'T IT BE FUNNY?

Wouldn't it be funny,
Wouldn't it now
If the dog said, "Moo,"
And the cow said, "Bow-wow,"
And the cat sang and whistled
And the bird said, "Meow"?
Wouldn't it be funny?
Wouldn't it now?

God often comforts us, not by changing the circumstances of our lives, but by changing our attitude toward them.

114

HOMES

Birds build a home in a bush or a tree,
And toads live under a stone.
But a spider weaves a beautiful web,
And ants make a hill all their own.
The turtle carries a house made of a shell;
The squirrel's home is a hole in a tree,
And fish dart about in water deep.
Each likes his own home, you see.
Homes for everyone—and my home for me.

Giving and receiving kindness is a far more effective way to learn than merely listening to words about kindness.

DANCE OF THE LEAVES

The autumn leaves are dancing down—
Dance, leaves, dance!
Leaves of crimson, gold and brown—
Dance, leaves, dance!

Let the wind whirl you around—
Make a carpet for the ground.
Soon you'll sleep without a sound—
Dance, leaves, dance!

COUNTING RHYMES

One, two, buckle my shoe
Three, four, shut the door
Five, six, pick up sticks
Seven, eight, lay them straight
Nine, ten, a big fat hen.

One, two, three, four, five,
I caught a hare alive;
Six, seven, eight, nine, ten,
I let it go again.

IF YOU EVER

If you ever ever ever ever ever,
    If you ever ever ever meet a whale,
You must never never never never never
    You must never never never touch its tail:
For if you ever ever ever ever ever
    If you ever ever ever touch its tail,
You will never never never never never
    You will never never meet another whale!

THE AIRPLANE

The airplane taxies down the field
And heads into the breeze.
It lifts its wheels above the ground,
And skims above the trees.
It rises high and higher
Away up toward the sun,
It's just a speck against the sky
—And now it's gone!

WHISTLE

I want to learn to whistle,
I've always wanted to;
I fix my mouth to do it, but
The whistle won't come through.

I think perhaps it's stuck, and so
I try it once again;
Can people swallow whistles?
Where is my whistle then?

THE ELEPHANT

The elephant walks like this and like that.
He's terribly big, and he's terribly fat!
He has no fingers, but he does have toes.
And goodness gracious!
What a nose!

LONG, LONG AGO

Winds through the olive trees
    Softly did blow,
Round little Bethlehem
    Long, long ago.
Sheep on the hillside lay
    Whiter than snow;
Shepherds were watching them,
    Long, long ago.
Then from the happy sky,
    Angels bent low,
Singing their songs of joy,
    Long, long ago.
For in a manger bed,
    Cradled we know,
Christ came to Bethlehem,
    Long, long ago.

Most of us have two chances of becoming wealthy — slim and none!

FATHER, WE THANK THEE

Father, we thank thee for the night
And for the pleasant morning light,
For rest and food and loving care,
And all that makes the world so fair.
Help us to do the things we should,
To be to others kind and good;
In all we do, in all we say
To grow more loving every day.

DID YOU KNOW that it would take 9,000 years to count to one billion?

Jed: "Your sister is spoiled, isn't she?"
Ted: "No, that's the perfume she uses."

"You look pretty dirty, Susie."
"Thank you. I look pretty when I'm clean, too."

117

Mother: "Eat your spinach. It will put color in your
　　　　cheeks."
Son: "Who wants green cheeks?"

Father: "Son, do you realize when Lincoln was your
　　　　age he was already studying hard to be a
　　　　lawyer?"
Son: "Right, pop, and when he was your age, he
　　　　was already President of the United States."

Tom: "What are you—animal, vegetable, or
　　　　mineral?"
Tim: "Vegetable. I'm a human bean!"

Q: "Which month has twenty-eight days?"
A: "They all have."

Q: "What do they call a man who steals ham?"
A: "A hamburglar."

Jill: "Did you hear the rope joke?"
Jack: "No."
Jill: "Skip it."

Bill: "Where does a sheep get his hair cut?"
Phil: "At the baa-baa shop, of course."

A six-year-old lad came home from school one day with a note from his teacher which suggested that he be taken out of school because he was "too stupid to learn." His name was Thomas Alva Edison.

Pat: "I'm studying gozinta in school."
Mike: "What in the world is gozinta?"
Pat: "You know gozinta. Two goes into four, four
　　　　goes into eight, eight goes into six-
　　　　teen . . . ."

Q: "What kind of animal can jump higher than a
　　　　house?"
A: "All kinds—a house can't jump at all!"

Q: "Why does a hummingbird hum?"
A: "Because he doesn't know the words."

118

Q: "What kind of bird is like a car?"
A: "A goose. They both honk."

Q: "What kind of room has no doors, no windows, and no walls?"
A: "A mushroom."

NAME THE FLOWER

What flower is part of an eye? (Iris)
What did Johnny do when he sat on a tack? (Rose)
What flower holds a dairy product? (Buttercup)
What flower is a country with lots of automobiles? (Carnation)

*When opportunity does knock
By some uncanny quirk
It often goes unrecognized —
It so resembles work!*

NAME THE TREE

What tree keeps a lady warm? (Fir)
What tree is a couple? (Pear)
What tree is part of your hand? (Palm)
What tree is near the sea? (Beech)

HINKY-PINKY

A hinky-pinky is a pair of rhyming definitions. For example, the hinky-pinky for a skinny young horse is a bony pony. A seafood platter is a fish dish. What would the following be?

You can no more blame your circumstances for your character than you can the mirror for your looks.

A tiny insect is a wee _ _ _ _. (flea)
A small frankfurter is a teeny _ _ _ _ _ _. (wienie)
Noah's unlighted boat is a _ _ _ _ _ _ _. (dark ark)
An angry employer is a cross _ _ _ _. (boss)
A happy father is a _ _ _ _ _ _ _. (glad dad)
A happy dog is a jolly _ _ _ _ _ _. (collie)
Make up some of your own hinky-pinky riddles.

119

BIBLE CHARACTER ALPHABET QUIZ

This is a reference-research game using a Bible. References are given for your child to check to get the answers to the questions.

Nick: "What instructions did Noah give his sons about fishing off the ark?"
Rick: "I don't know."
Nick: "Go easy on the bait, boys. I only have two worms."

1. A___ ___ ___ ___ ___ ___ ___ was a monarch who reigned in the East (Esther 1:1).
2. B___ ___ ___ ___ ___ ___ ___ ___ was a king who made a great feast (Daniel 5:1-4).
3. C___ ___ ___ ___ was truthful when others told lies (Numbers 13:30-33).
4. D___ ___ ___ ___ ___ ___ was a woman, heroic and wise (Judges 4:4-14).
5. E___ ___ ___ ___ ___ was a refuge where David spared Saul (1 Samuel 24:1-7).
6. F___ ___ ___ ___ ___ was a Roman, accuser of Paul (Acts 26:24).
7. G___ ___ ___ ___ ___ ___ ___ ___ ___ was a garden where Jesus prayed (Matthew 26:36).
8. H___ ___ ___ ___ ___ was a city where King David stayed (2 Samuel 2:11).
9. I___ ___ ___ ___ ___ ___ was a mocker (Genesis 21:9).
10. J___ ___ ___ ___ ___ ___ ___ ___ was a city, preferred above joy (Psalm 137:6).
11. K___ ___ ___ was a father whose son was quite tall (1 Samuel 9:1-2).
12. L___ ___ ___ ___ ___ ___ was a proud one who had a great fall (Isaiah 14:12, KJV).
13. M___ ___ ___ was a nephew whose uncle was good (Colossians 4:10).
14. N___ ___ ___ ___ ___ ___ was a city, long hid where it stood (Zephaniah 2:13).
15. P___ ___ ___ was a Christian, greeting another (2 Timothy 1:1, 2).
16. R___ ___ ___ ___ was a servant girl who knew Peter's voice (Acts 12:13, 14).
17. S___ ___ ___ ___ ___ ___ was a king who sat on a throne (1 Kings 1:46).

18. T _ _ _ _ was a seaport where preaching was long (Acts 20:6, 7).
19. U _ _ _ _ was a teamster, struck dead for his wrong (2 Samuel 6:7).
20. V _ _ _ _ _ was a castoff, and never restored (Esther 1:19).
21. Z _ _ _ was a ruin with sorrow deplored (Psalm 137:1).

ANSWERS:

21. Zion	14. Nineveh	7. Gethsemane
20. Vashti	13. Mark	6. Festus
19. Uzzah	12. Lucifer	5. En Gedi
18. Troas	11. Kish	4. Deborah
17. Solomon	10. Jerusalem	3. Caleb
16. Rhoda	9. Ishmael	2. Belshazzar
15. Paul	8. Hebron	1. Ahasuerus

Woman to her four-year-old grandson: "I can't kiss you with that dirty face." "That," said the boy, "is what I figured."

FLANNEL BOX. Cover the inside of a cigar box or pencil box with flannel. The outside of the box can be decorated with paint or other material. Cut pictures of people, animals, etc., from magazines and paste a piece of felt to the back of each. These can be stored in the bottom of the box. Your child now has a mini-flannelgraph kit for his own use in telling or making up new stories. He can put various figures on the flannel lid to illustrate the stories. The flannel-backed pictures will cling to the flannel lid.

STATES ABBREVIATED. Arkansas is the best state to be in during a flood because its abbreviation is ARK. And Illinois is the unhealthiest state to be in because its abbreviation is ILL. See if you can answer the following questions by filling each blank with the proper abbreviation.
What is the most selfish state? _ _ (Me.)
What is the cleanest state? _ _ _ _ (Wash.)
What is the father of states? _ _ (Pa.)
What is the doctor's state? _ _ (Md.)
What state never fails? _ _ _ (Kan.)

121

TONGUE TWISTERS. How fast can you say them? She sells seashells by the seashore. A noise annoys an oyster. Peter Piper picked a peck of pickled peppers.

ACTION AND RHYMES AND FINGER PLAYS

Springtime is the wake-up time

For birds and trees

      and flowers;

God sends the rain

and sunshine down

      to make this world of ours.

God never put anyone in a place too small to grow.

I'm all made of hinges

And everything bends,

From the top of my head

'Way down to the ends.

I'm hinges in front,

I'm hinges in back;

If I didn't have hinges,

I surely would crack!

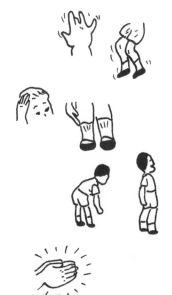

122

This is the church,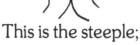

This is the steeple;

Open the doors,

And see all the people.

First they sing,

Then they pray;

And then they quietly walk away.

I'll touch my head,
my hair,
my hand;
I'll sit up straight,
and then I'll stand!
I'll touch my ears,
my nose,
my chin,
Then quietly sit down again.

For I am convinced that neither death nor life, neither angels nor demons, neither the present nor the future to come, nor any powers, neither height nor depth, nor anything else in all creation, will be able to separate us from the love of God that is in Christ Jesus our Lord.
—Romans 8:38-39

BIBLE ARITHMETIC

Add to the number of silver pieces for which Jesus
was sold. (Matthew 26:15)
The sum of days Jesus was seen after his death.
(Acts 1:3).
And the age of Jesus when he began his ministry
(Luke 3:23).
Divide this by the number of silver pieces a woman
had (Luke 15:8).
Subtract from this the number of commandments
on which hang all the law of the prophets
(Matthew 22:36-40).
You will have the victory chapter of Romans.
What chapter is it? (8)

*If you don't enjoy what
you have now, how could
you be happier with
more?*

Take the number of years that the Israelites
tempted God (Hebrews 3:9).
Divide this by the number of lepers Jesus cleansed
at one time (Luke 17:17)
Add to this the number of angels that were seen at
the tomb of Jesus (Luke 24:4).
You will have the number of the chapter in Matthew where the Lord's Prayer is located.
What chapter is it? (6)

SEEING STARS AND STRIPES! Draw an
American flag on a large piece of paper. Make the
stripes green and black, and color the stars orange
or gold. Stare at the flag for several minutes without
looking away. Then look at a blank wall. On the wall
you will see the American flag in red, white, and
blue! What happened? If you look at one color long
enough, you will see its complementary color.
White is the complement of black, red is the complement of green, and orange is the complement of
blue.

CRAZY PICS look quite strange. Can you figure out what each picture is? Draw some crazy pics of your own.

1.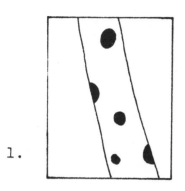

2.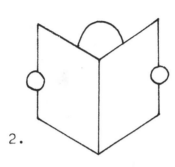

3.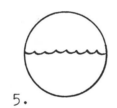

4.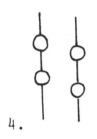

5.

6.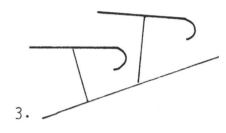

7.

PAINTS, CRAYONS, CLAY, GLUE, AND OTHER GOOEY STUFF

CHAPTER 9

The righteous man leads a blameless life; blessed are his children after him.
—Proverbs 20:7

Perhaps the most challenging task of any generation is the religious nurture of its children. This is a great opportunity and responsibility. If parents are able to nurture a vital religious experience within the child, they are laying the foundations for the social and moral convictions of a lifetime.

Religious growth is a gradual process. Like the unfolding of a plant, it is a matter of first the seed, then the ear, then the full grain. The child's experiences in finding religious meanings in life must be vivid and personal. Furthermore, he needs much time to make his individual discoveries.

God is not revealed by definitions, nor does a vocabulary of religious phrases and Bible passages guarantee Christian thought and behavior. Religion is not a topic, but a life. You can't fully explain it. You do not only teach it. You let it grow. Tolerance, goodness, love, and reverence develop in children when they sense these qualities in those around them.

Tolerance is perhaps one attribute that we can nurture in ourselves as we allow childhood experimentation in art and craft activities. Goodness and

126

love shine through as we encourage this experimentation.

What a privilege to help children grow in positive behavior, confidence, and independence. Your "I believe you can do it" attitude will encourage children to have self-confidence in their ideas and skills.

Art allows young children to express themselves at a stage when they are still largely nonverbal. In art activities the child faces a great many choices: Which color shall I use? Where shall I place my figures? How large should they be? What should they look like? For someone who has little say about the things that happen to him, these opportunities can help build self-confidence.

It is not possible to grade most activities as suitable or unsuitable in themselves for any given age. Activities must be judged in the light of the underlying motivation. Even the simplest activity, such as pasting or cutting, may become necessary to the working out of a larger project by older boys and girls. For instance, if we say that cutting and pasting is a respectable activity for a kindergarten age child, but not for a teenager, we miss the point. Just watch a teenage boy—a baseball enthusiast—making his own baseball scrapbook with countless pictures and clippings cut from newspapers and magazines and pasted in with meticulous care, and you realize that he has no aversion to cutting and pasting. This fits into his own purposes and is a part of some larger end which he wants to achieve.

Motivation is basic in creative activities. Activities that are similar in themselves may be different in value because one is merely "handwork" and nothing more, while the other is the expression of a definite purpose.

Don't judge children's art by adult standards—the greatest block to youthful creativeness. Don't ask children, "What is that?" The child may not have thought about a concrete object until you

Always be tolerant with the person who disagrees with you. After all, he has a right to his ridiculous opinions.

asked him. And thinking about a real object may get in the way of the feelings he was trying to express or the experimenting he was doing. He may just be satisfied with the mushing, sloshing, and manipulating of materials, rather than in comments on the artwork itself. It is best to make a general comment like, "You're really enjoying yourself today, aren't you?"

The possibility of experimenting in artwork is great and as the child does so, he also answers scientific questions that we take for granted: What happens to colors when they are mixed? How does paint change when it is mixed with water? What happens to clay when squished through fingers?

Be selective about making models for children to copy even if the child asks you to. If you do, you are again setting standards that may be too high as well as making it more difficult for children to use their own imagination.

Be prepared for a mess with art and craft projects. Be sure to put newspapers around the work area. Provide damp paper towels for cleanup and for washing hands throughout messy projects. A little time spent in adequate preparation beforehand prevents a possible situation of unhappiness later on if a mess is made where no protection was provided.

When you row the other fellow across the stream, you get there yourself.

SAND CASTING. You will need: sand, water, shoe box, paper clips, stones and other small objects, plaster of paris. Fill the box half full with moist sand. Poke designs in the sand with your finger, a stick, or other object. Place small objects upside down in the sand. Pour one inch of plaster of paris over entire sand surface. Before it sets, insert a paper clip at the top for a hanger. After plaster has hardened, gently lift the casting out of the box and brush off excess sand. The plaster cast can be painted with tempera or watercolors.

ME-DOLL. Obtain an old sheet. Trace around the child with a felt pen as he or she lies on the sheet. Draw two patterns—one for front, one for back. Put newspapers under the sheet. Using crayons or felt pens, let the child color the pattern to look like himself—clothes, hair, and eyes. Now cut out the two patterns. Sew the two pieces together, leaving an opening on one side. Stuff the doll with scrap material, wadded newspaper, cotton, or foam. Sew the opening closed. You now have a life-size doll that looks like your child!

MAKE PASTING EASIER for young children by placing a dab of paste on a 3 x 5 inch piece of waxed paper. Provide a popsicle stick to apply the paste.

slits

FOAM CUPS can be turned into flowers—or into an octupus! Children need help with this project. Cut slits about halfway down the sides of a foam cup, about ½ to 1 inch apart. Hold the cup upside down over very low heat of an electric burner (DO NOT TOUCH BURNER.) (DO NOT USE OPEN FLAME!). The tabs will curl up creating an open flower or the arms of an octopus. For a flower, attach chenille wire stems and construction paper leaves. The cups can be glued to a sheet of construction paper to make 3-D bouquet.

ROLL PAINTING. Collect empty roll-on deodorant bottles. Pinch off the roll-tops and wash them and the bottles thoroughly. Fill the bottles with liquid tempera paint. Snap the roll-tops back in place. Use the bottles as you would a brush to create exciting bright-colored pictures. When you are finished painting, cover the bottles with their original lids.

3-D PICTURES. Dip into your box of scraps for things you can use to make three-dimensional pictures. Paper cups cut in half from top to bottom, paper plates, tiny boxes, fabric, etc., can be used effectively. Glue the items onto paper to create interesting 3-D effects.

PAPER LOOP and strip pictures are similar to the 3-D pictures described above. Cut strips of paper about one inch wide and in varying lengths. Some of the strips can be made into loops while others can be used as straight strips. Paste the pieces at random onto a sheet of construction paper to make an interesting design.

PAPER LOOP ANIMALS. Cut one-inch strips of paper into varying lengths. Paste the ends of each strip together to make loops. Now paste the various loops together to make animals and other figures. Use larger loops for bodies, smaller for heads, hands, feet, ears, etc.

BLEACH PAINTING. Pour a small amount of household bleach into a cup. You might want to make a hole in the cap of a small jar just large enough to insert a cotton swab. Dip a cotton swab into the bleach and paint a picture on colored construction paper. As the bleach begins to dry, you will see the color disappearing from the paper. Your picture will show up in light lines on the darker paper. KEEP THE BLEACH AWAY FROM MOUTH AND EYES! Wear some protective garment, such as a paint shirt, to keep the bleach from getting on your clothes.

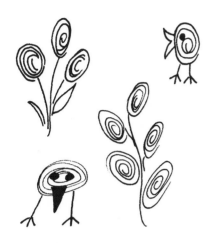

THUMBPRINT PICTURES. Put a bit of liquid tempera or watercolor paint onto a paper towel so that it soaks in a bit. Press your thumb down onto the towel to get some paint on it, as if you were having your fingerprint taken. Then press your thumb down onto another sheet of paper. Keep making the thumbprints until you have enough to make a picture. Now, using a crayon or felt pen, draw additional lines or details to make your picture complete.

MASKING TAPE LEATHER LOOK. Tear masking tape into bits and pieces and stick them all over the outside of a bottle, box, or other object you want to cover. Make sure the tape bits overlap so that the entire surface is covered. Paint over the tape with brown shoe polish. When the polish dries, the item will have a leather appearance. Bottles or jars make attractive vases.

FOAM EGG CARTON CHARACTERS. With a few snips of the scissors you can make whimsical characters from foam egg cartons. Cut the foam into small triangular pieces and paste them together in the shape of an animal, flower, etc., on a piece of construction paper.

GLASS PAINTING. You will need a small picture frame with glass and cardboard, a piece of felt or terry cloth the same size as the glass, paper and pencil, tempera paint, and a small paintbrush. On paper, draw or trace a picture smaller than the frame. Lay the glass over the picture. Then trace the picture with tempera on the glass. Glue the corners of the fabric to the glass on the same side on which you painted. Now place the glass and fabric into the frame and replace the cardboard backing. Your picture is ready to hang.

COOKIE CUTTER SOAPS. You will need pieces of leftover soap, assorted cookie cutters, a cookie sheet, spatula, large spoon, double boiler, paper towels. Boil water in the lower part of the double boiler. Put soap pieces and a little water in the top part and set over the boiling water. As the soap warms and softens, use the spoon to smooth out any lumps, adding a bit more water if necessary. The mixture should not be thin (the soap will take longer to dry out if it is). When the soap has softened to the consistency of thick oatmeal, turn it out on a cookie sheet, smoothing and stretching it. It should be about ⅜ inch thick.

Allow it to cool and harden a few minutes. Then cut shapes with the cookie cutters. Remove the soap shapes from the pan with a spatula and place them on paper towels to dry. Gather up the soap scraps and mold them into soap balls. Allow the soap to harden at least overnight. You may want to experiment with the addition of food coloring as the soap is being softened. These soaps make unusual gifts. If you want to collect soap scraps for a while until you get enough to work with, store the pieces in a covered container with a bit of water. This will start the softening process.

"You shouldn't worry like that. It doesn't do any good."
"It does for me! Ninety percent of the things I worry about never happen!"

The people we have the most trouble with is ourselves.

TISSUE PAPER COLLAGE. Arrange tissue paper cut out or torn in various shapes and colors on one piece of waxed paper. Cover with another piece of waxed paper the same size. Put plain paper under and over the waxed paper and press with a warm iron. Remove the plain paper and you will have a sealed collage that can be hung up for display.

SILK SCREEN GREETING CARDS. Make a screen by stretching some thin transparent material, such as an old nylon stocking, over an embroidery hoop and fasten it tightly with a rubber band. On a sheet of paper the same size as the hoop, draw the outline of the design you want to use on the greeting cards. Place the hoop upside down over the sketch and outline the drawing on the fabric with a dark colored crayon, pressing down heavily. Place the screen over the greeting card paper and pour thick tempera or finger paint onto the screen. Use a match folder or a piece of cardboard as a squeegee to pull the paint across the screen. The paint will pass through the fabric everywhere except on the crayoned design. The process can be repeated to make many cards in a variety of colors.

The finest of all gifts are not things but opportunities.

SOAPY CREATURES. Pour some soap flakes into a large container. Add water slowly until the mixture is the consistency of paste. Roll it into balls. Put the balls together with toothpicks to create figures, such as a snowman or an animal. Use chenille wire pieces for arms on the snowman. When you are ready to discard the figure, the toothpicks and other material can be removed and the balls used for hand soap.

TIN CAN WIND CHIMES. You will need a large and a small tin can with just one end removed. The small can should be small enough to rattle around inside the larger can. Be sure the cans are clean and have no sharp edges. Using lacquer or enamel, paint designs on the cans. When they are dry, punch a hole in the center of the end of each can with a nail and hammer. Cut a long piece of heavy string or cord. Fold the cord in half and tie the ends together in a big knot. Push the looped end inside the small can and pull it all the way through the hole. Tie another knot in the cord, placing it so the large can cannot slide all the way down over the small can. Push the loop inside the large can and pull it through the hole. Tie a knot in the cord just on top of the can. Hang the wind chime outside where the wind will blow it.

FOAM CITY. Cut house, building, tree, car, people, etc., shapes from pieces of Styrofoam which is about one inch thick. The shapes will be able to stand and can be arranged to make a city to use with your model train or other toys. Some patterns for these pieces are in chapter 10.

The best way to make children good is to make them happy.   —Wilde

PLACE a piece of wet sponge inside the lid of a jar of paste or play dough to keep it moist between uses.

TAPE a cuffed bag to the edge of the table for scraps while your child is cutting paper.

SHOE BOX TOTEM POLES. Turn recycled shoe boxes into unique totem poles. You do not need the box tops. Paint or draw faces and other features on the bottoms and sides of the boxes. Use scrap paper or cardboard to make wings, ears, or beaks to glue onto the boxes. Stack the boxes end to end and glue them together to construct the totem poles.

Weeds and grain grow in the same surroundings— the only difference seems to be in their parents.

BURLAP WALL HANGINGS. Wall hangings can be colorful and highly decorative. You will need: a 12 by 15 inch piece of burlap, colored felt scraps, a dowel stick, a cord, pins, paper, glue, scissors, and pencil. Draw or trace a picture or design. Cut out the parts of the design and pin these pieces to the felt scraps. Cut the felt pieces around the patterns. Remove the paper patterns. Glue the felt pieces to the burlap to create your design. Insert the dowel stick through a hem in the top of the burlap. Cut a piece of cord the desired length and tie it to both ends of the dowel for a hanger.

SCRAP WOOD SCULPTURE. Obtain wood scraps of various sizes and shapes. Glue them together to create a free-standing design sculpture. The sculpture can be painted if you wish.

GEOMETRIC CUTTING. Interesting designs can be created by cutting geometric shapes in a piece of paper. The trick is that the shape is not entirely cut from the paper but left attached on one side. The cut part is then folded up from the paper giving a raised effect. Experiment with cutting various shapes and design arrangements. You can paste a contrasting color of paper underneath it to add more interest to the design. To cut the following designs, cut on the solid lines and fold on the dotted lines.

PAPER PLATE AND EGG CARTON MASKS. Turn a paper plate right side up. Cut egg cups from an egg carton and paste them around the edge of the upper half of the plate for hair. Paste one egg cup in the middle of the plate for a nose. Cut holes in the plate for eyes and a mouth. Paint the plate, hair, etc. Attach a piece of yarn or string to each side to tie the mask on with. Paste scrap materials, buttons, paper loops, foam packing pieces, etc., to the inside of the lid of an egg carton to create another type of mask.

PAPER LOG CABINS. Tightly roll pieces of paper lengthwise to make "logs." Newspaper pieces are good for this activity. Pieces of paper about 9 by 5 inches in size work well. After you have several rolled logs, paste them together to build a log cabin. Fold a piece of cardboard in half to make a roof. Paste a cardboard rectangle to the front of the cabin for a door.

A little explained,
        A little endured,
A little forgiven,
        The quarrel is cured.

DESIGN a family "crest" or "coat-of-arms." Determine details about your family you want to include in the design. Draw the design on paper, color it, and hang it up. You might want to transfer the design to a piece of fabric and stitch or embroider it, then have it framed.

MARBLE PAPER. Wet a piece of paper by dipping it in a pan of water. Paint on it large spots of watercolor. Crumple the paper in your hand, squeezing out surplus water. Open it and let it dry. This paper makes fine book covers.

BATIK. Materials: Any fabric that will take wax crayon coloring and dye well, crayons, wax or paraffin, dye. With crayons, color sections of the material, going in different directions with different colors. When the area is covered, press with a warm iron between old newspapers. Put black silhouette picture or block letters on the piece, using black crayon, coloring very heavy and solid. Press again to get wax from the material.

You may stop here, or you may obtain a water crackle finish by painting melted wax over the whole piece. When completely covered, run cold water over the piece; then crumple the piece in your hands and dip into a pan of dye of any color that will go well with the background colors. Let drip. Then press again between sheets of newspaper to remove the wax. If this is to be a wall hanging, hem sides and top; fringe bottom by pulling crosswise threads. Run a dowel stick through top hem and fasten a pretty cord or yarn to ends and hand. Or make scarves or aprons.

Money will buy a bed but not sleep; books but not brains; food but not appetite; finery but not beauty; medicine but not health; luxury but not culture; amusement but not happiness; a big church but not salvation!

136

SALT BEADS
    2 parts table salt
    1 part flour
    water
    coloring

Mix salt and flour and water to doughlike consistency. Add coloring. Break off pieces and form into beads. Pierce each bead with a toothpick and allow to dry. These can be strung on thread or string to make necklaces and bracelets.

YARN POM-POMS. Lay a short piece of yarn along the bottom edge of a one-inch cardboard strip. Then wrap yarn 25 times around the cardboard strip. With the short piece, gather the loops together and tie tightly, removing the cardboard at the same time. Cut loops and clip ends to make a soft puff. Sew them together to make interesting figures.

1.

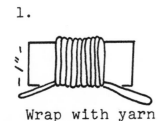

Wrap with yarn

2.

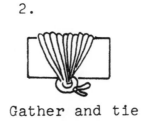

Gather and tie

3.

Cut loops at top

PUFF BASKETBALL. Cut the bottom out of a lunch-size paper bag and fasten it to a wall or door. Use the pom-poms described above and you have a nice indoor basketball game.

PAPER FLOWERS. Patterns for various paper flowers are in chapter 10. Trace the patterns onto construction paper. Cut them out and paste together. Chenille wire can be used for stems so the flowers will stand in a vase.

MAKE AN EASEL. An easel may be inexpensively made like the sketch. For legs, use lumber approximately ¾ by 1½ inches by 50 inches long. You will need four of these. The backboard should be either 20 by 26 inches or 24 by 30 inches. This may be plywood. The base of the board should be 26 inches from the floor. Below this attach a shallow tray wide enough to hold baby food jars for paint. Put hinges at the top so that the easel can be folded together for storage. Put a backboard on each side to make a two-sided easel. Spring clips or clothespins can be used to hold paper to the board when painting.

TABLETOP EASEL. Cut away part of a cardboard box to make this tabletop easel. It will be handy to use when you are painting a picture. Attach your paper to a piece of heavy cardboard and stand it up on the easel. The easel can also be used for displaying your paintings.

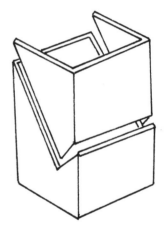

What makes it hard to live on today's income are neighbors who don't.

RECIPES for various types of modeling clay, paste, and paints are included in chapter 10. There are also simple patterns that can be used with your art and craft activities.

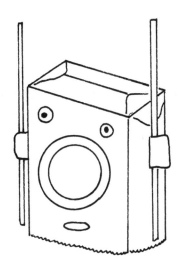

PAPER BAG MASKS. You will need ordinary brown paper bags, glue, scraps of yarn, soda straws, paints or crayons, and construction paper. For each mask cut out little slits or holes for your eyes and nose. Decorate the bags by glueing on features cut from construction paper (yarn for hair, etc.) to make the face you want. Here are some samples. The spaceman mask has cellophane glued behind the hole. Cut a hole beneath it for air. Patterns for some attachments are in chapter 10.

FLOWER DRYING. Place small leaves and flowers between pages of old magazines or old telephone books and put a heavy weight on top. If you use a regular book be sure to put waxed paper around the flower so that book isn't stained. After several days they should be flat and dry.

Make fancy notepaper from your dried flowers. Determine the size of notepaper you want to use. A sheet of colored paper about 5 by 8 inches in size is usually large enough for notes. Cut a piece of clear Con-Tact the same size as your notepaper. Lay your dried flowers in a design on one half of the sticky side of the Con-Tact. Now lay the piece of colored paper over them. Press it down well to remove all the air bubbles from under the Con-Tact. Fold the paper in half and you have a pretty piece of notepaper to use when you write to a friend.

BREAD DOUGH PICTURES. Remove the crust from a loaf of white bread. Break the bread into tiny pieces in a bowl. Add a little white glue and begin mixing it into the bread with a spoon or fork. Keep adding small amounts of glue until you get a very stiff dough. It will be a bit sticky to the touch. Take little pieces of the dough to make flower petals, leaves, and stems. Just put the pieces together to make a flower. They will stick. Lay the flowers on a sheet of waxed paper until dry. They will harden and can be painted with tempera paint. If you wish, you can add a tiny bit of food coloring to the glue before you mix it with the bread. You can make other figures from the dough such as people, animals, letters, vehicles, etc. These figures can be glued to a stiff backing to be hung for display.

Don't wait for moods. You accomplish nothing if you do that. Your mind must know it has to get down to work. **—Pearl Buck**

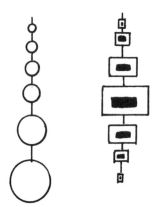

MOBILES. Interesting mobiles can be made from various sized and colored geometric shapes. Use fine thread to tie the pieces together, then hang them from a branch or coat hanger to blow freely in the air.

Be strong in the Lord and in his mighty power. Put on the full armor of God so that you can take your stand against the devil's schemes.
—Ephesians 6:10-11

PATTERNS, RECIPES, AND WHAT TO DO WHEN ALL ELSE FAILS

CHAPTER 10

But as for me and my household, we will serve the Lord. —*Joshua 24:15*

Children need a sense of trust from caring adults: assurance, a pat on the back, comfort, a helping hand over a new high hurdle. All children will need it now and then. Some will need it more than others. You cannot measure it out in even doses. Nor can you sit like a judge on high and say: "You have had enough. You should not want any more."

If you have any doubts remember: a youngster cannot feel strong with an empty spot inside. No matter how old your children are, support them when they want you to. Comfort them when they need you. Stand by them when they want you near. When they ask for your helping hand, give it to them. This will not make them soft; it will give them the courage to grow.

When your children were infants and cried, you held them. Now when they are sad, comfort them. Their crying tells you that they want some loving; their relaxation and happiness and peace tell you that you are right when you give it to them. Children who sense fully your friendly support move naturally on to the next stage in their growth.

When you let your children know you have

confidence in their abilities and ideas, you are demonstrating to them your love and understanding. Then they begin to feel a bit of God's love for them as it is expressed through you, one of God's people.

Treat a child as he is and he will remain as he is; but treat him as he could, should, and might be, then he will strive to become the kind of person you convey to him.
—William Moore, Jr.

ENCOURAGE your child to plan his day's activities. He can prepare a monthly or weekly calendar and list or draw pictures of things he would like to do on the different days. Or he can use the calendar to keep track of the things he has already done each day. This will help him understand that we have only a limited amount of time to do all the things we want and need to do, and the importance of structuring our time so that we accomplish the things we plan.

PERK up your child's day by arranging for her to receive some mail when the mailman comes to the house. Send her a note or postcard just to let her know you love her. You might put a riddle in the note, suggest a project to do that day, or write a little prayer she can memorize. It is quite exciting to be little and still have the mailman bring something just for you!

SALT AND FLOUR RELIEF MAP. To two cups of salt and one cup of flour add enough water to make a stiff paste. Outline a map on heavy cardboard or plywood, noting the topography of the land—mountains, lakes, plains, rivers. Spread the clay over the drawn outline, building it up for mountains, leveling it off for the plains. Leave empty spaces for lakes and rivers. Allow the map to dry for a few days. Then it can be painted with tempera paint—blue for bodies of water, green for plains, brown for mountains, with perhaps some white snow on the top of higher peaks.

142

PAINT FOR ROCKS. Mix some liquid starch with powdered tempera paint to a smooth consistency. This makes a bright paint that adheres well to rocks.

Q: "How did Jonah feel when the great fish swallowed him?"
A: "Down in the mouth."

MODELING CLAY
    1 cup flour
    ½ cup salt
    1 teaspoon powdered alum
    water or glycerin for mixing
Mix thoroughly, then mix with water or glycerin to consistency desired. Color with food coloring.

PAPER PULP CLAY
    shredded newspapers
    boiling water
    2 cups flour
    ½ cup salt
Tear newspapers into small pieces and cover with boiling water. Allow to soak for 24 hours. Stir or beat into a pulp. Drain off water and strain pulp through cheesecloth. Add two cups flour and one-half cup salt to each three cups of pulp. Knead like bread dough until the mixture reaches the consistency of putty. Cover with a damp cloth. This clay will be an excellent substitute for store-bought modeling clay.

SAWDUST MODELING CLAY
    4 cups fine sawdust
    1 cup water
    2 cups wheat flour
        (wallpaper paste)
Mix together. Produces a very pliable clay. Use like dough although it is not as firm a consistency.

SODA AND CORNSTARCH CLAY

1 cup cornstarch
1¼ cups water
2 cups baking soda
food coloring

Combine first three ingredients and cook over medium heat stirring constantly. When mixture is thickened to a doughlike consistency, turn out on a piece of foil. Food coloring may be kneaded into the clay when cooled slightly. Store in a plastic bag in the refrigerator.

Inspiration is far more likely to strike a busy person than an idle person.

FINGER PAINT

1 cup flour
1 cup liquid detergent
1 cup water
food coloring

Mix until creamy and lumps are gone. This makes 2 cups of creamy paint. For a foamy paint which makes about 50 percent more bulk, use 2 cups water and cook with the flour, stirring vigorously until smooth and thick. Add detergent and coloring, and beat with an eggbeater.

FOAM STUCCO. To two parts of soap or detergent, flakes or granules, add one part of water. Add vegetable coloring if desired. Whip until very stiff. Laundry starch may be used in place of water to above mixture to make a harder material when dried. This will look like plaster. Spread it with a knife on the article to be decorated. It is a good covering for Bible-times houses which you make out of cardboard.

GLAZE. Mix two parts white glue to one part water. Brush it over other painted surfaces for a shiny finish.

CORNSTARCH PAINT

    3 tablespoons cornstarch
    1 pint water
    coloring (vegetable or tempera)

Mix 3 level tablespoons of cornstarch with part of the pint of water. Boil remainder of pint, add starch mixture stirring until clear. Remove from heat. After starch paint is cool, add the coloring. Store in baby food jars. This is excellent for poster painting.

FINGER PAINT

    1 quart water
    1 tablespoon flour
    3 tablespoons starch
    tempera or vegetable coloring
    few drops wintergreen oil

Add a small amount of water to the starch and flour to make a paste. Boil the rest of the water and add the paste. Cook until thick, adding a few drops of oil of wintergreen to keep paint from forming scum. Stir to keep smooth. Add color. Store in baby food jars.

*Though thy name be
   spread abroad,
Like winged seed from
   shore to shore,
What thou art before thy
   God,
That thou art and nothing
   more.*

CHRISTMAS DECORATIONS

    1 cup salt
    ½ cup cornstarch
    ½ cup boiling water

Mix dry ingredients thoroughly. Pour boiling water on mixture while stirring vigorously. Keep over fire until mixture forms a dough. Then knead until the mixture reaches the consistency of bread dough. Roll out thin on waxed paper. Cut into desired shapes and cover with a moist cloth. Cookie cutters are great for making the different shapes. Punch small holes with a pencil or nail for attaching strings. Drying takes about 12 hours. If turned two or three times while drying, edges will not curl. When dry, paint on designs. Or cover with thin film of glue and sprinkle on some glitter. Tie ribbon strings through the holes and hang them on your tree.

SPARKLING MODELING CLAY

2 cups salt
1 cup cornstarch
2/3 cup water
½ cup cold water

Mix salt and 2/3 cup water in saucepan. Place pan over low heat and stir mixture constantly until it is thoroughly heated (about 3 or 4 minutes). Remove from heat. Immediately mix cornstarch and ½ cup cold water. Add this at once to the hot salt mixture. Stir quickly to combine. Mixture should become thick like stiff dough. If mixture does not thicken, place pan over low heat again and stir hard about a minute or until mixture starts to thicken. When it cools, turn the clay out on a breadboard or other flat surface and begin modeling.

Figures will dry and harden at room temperature in about 36 hours. To speed drying, preheat oven to 350 degrees. Turn oven off and place figures on a wire rack to allow air circulation. Leave in oven until it is cold. When dry, the surfaces may be smoothed by rubbing with fine sandpaper or an emery board. To store the clay, wrap it in plastic or foil and keep it in a tightly closed container. Hundreds of tiny sparkles will appear when the clay dries.

Experience is a wonderful thing. It enables you to recognize a mistake when you make it again.

PASTE. One cup sugar, one cup flour, four cups warm water, one teaspoon powdered alum, a few drops oil of wintergreen. Mix dry ingredients in top of double boiler. Add water slowly, stirring continuously. Cook until clear, and a little longer. Remove from heat, add oil of wintergreen, mixing thoroughly. Cool. Place in jars. Cover. Will keep for several months in refrigerator. Makes about one quart of paste.

ADD powdered detergent to a cup of liquid tempera to help the paint adhere to the waxy surfaces of cottage cheese or milk cartons, etc.

146

RECYCLE old blue jeans into storage bags for toys, shoes, tools, etc. Patches can be decorated with felt and sewn on with colorful yarn. Slide a wooden dowel through the back belt loops and hang the jeans-bag by tying colorful heavy shoe strings or cord to the ends of the dowel. A wire coat hanger can also be used for hanging.

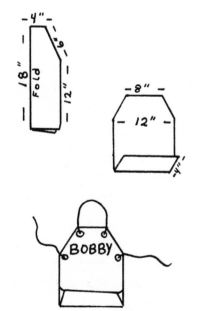

— original pockets

— slit for pockets
— pockets
— hand-stitched to close pockets

— patches
— slit for pockets

— hand-stitched to close

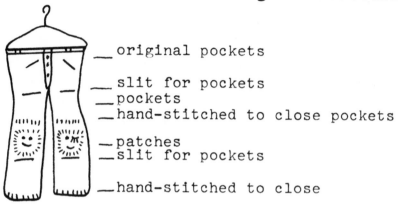

PAPIER-MÂCHÉ. Shred newspaper into a large plastic bucket and let it soak in water until it is reduced to a pulpy mass. Make a thick paste of flour, water, and a small quantity of salt in a separate container. Mix this paste with the paper mash. Stir until the mixture has the consistency of modeling clay. It is now ready for use. Make modeling frames by bending chicken wire into desired shapes, glueing pieces of wood into desired shapes, or using old light bulbs for round shapes. Spread the papier-mâché over the frame and smooth it out. Let it dry thoroughly. The figure can now be painted and put on display.

WORK APRON. Use a 12 by 18 inch piece of fabric. Cut it according to the pattern. Stitch around the edges. Fold up the bottom 4 inches and stitch to make a pocket. Attach a neck strap and ties made from heavy cord. Your child's name can be stitched or drawn on the front of the apron.

ACTION WORDS. Let your child run off a little energy by asking him or her to act out certain words like "jump," "fall down," "stand up," "clap," etc. Do a few action words at a time when there are long periods of passive activity. It will perk up the day and brighten the situation a bit.

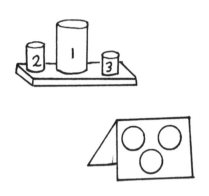

BEANBAGS are great for indoor play. Cut off the end of an old mitten or sock and fill with beans. Then sew the open end shut. Stand behind a line and toss the beanbag to the target. A wastebasket can be used for a target or you might want to make a more elaborate one as follows.

Glue cans or boxes of various sizes to a board. Number them, marking the higher scores on the smaller containers. You might also fold a piece of cardboard so that it stands up. Then cut holes in it for the targets. A pattern for a fish beanbag is included in the patterns at the end of this chapter.

INDOOR PICNIC. When spring rains keep you indoors for a few days, turn the living room into a "grassy knoll" and have a picnic at home! Use pictures of trees, flowers, and hills from magazines for atmosphere, or have your child draw some outdoor pictures. Eat, sing, play a game, and take a pretend nap. As you rest, thank God out loud for the happy time inside and for the rain outside.

worn toweling
sewn on

OLD SOCKS, with extra layers of worn-out toweling sewn to the bottom, make good silencers for children to wear if you have floors without carpets. They also make good house slippers. The slippers can fit over shoes and absorb much of the sound of marching, jumping, and running. Sew colorful felt designs or faces on the fronts of the socks for decoration. They are washable and cost you nothing but the time to make them.

KEEP a small plastic pail or box to collect small items that are found around the house during the day. Your child can put the things away when it is clean-up time.

A CURE for the midwinter blahs could be rearranging the children's room. Ask for their ideas. Is this the most convenient arrangement? Can they think of better ways? What would make the rooms more comfortable? More practical? More attractive? What can we get rid of?

When you sit and do nothing, you are sitting on the lid of the box that holds the answer to your problems.

FINGER PAINT. Mix one cup of Linit or Niagara starch with enough water to make a smooth paste. Add 5 cups of boiling water and cook until glossy. Cool slightly. Add one-half cup of Ivory Soap flakes while mixture is still warm. Beat with a beater. Divide into portions and color with powered tempera.

PARAFFIN COATING. Heat paraffin and a little mineral oil over very low heat, watching it constantly. When the paraffin is melted, let it cool a bit. Brush the mixture on pictures or dip leaves and other objects into it. This will preserve the items so they can be handled without getting soiled or without drying out.

WINDOW PAINT. One cup Bon Ami, one cup Alabastrine (glass paint or whiting), one cup dry tempera paint, water. Add enough water to the mixture of ingredients to make a paste. Paint the mixture on the window with a brush or rag. The paint is easily washed off the window with a damp cloth.

PLAY DOUGH. Two cups flour, one cup salt, two tablespoons olive oil, food coloring. Add water slowly to make a pliable mixture. Knead the ingredients together and place in a plastic bag or plastic container with a tight fitting lid. Keep it in the refrigerator when not being used.

PLAY CLAY. One cup flour, ½ cup salt, one tablespoon salad oil, two teaspoons cream of tartar, one cup water, food coloring. Cook over a low fire for about three minutes stirring constantly. When cooked to a dough consistency, it will pull away from the pan like a cream puff paste. Remove from the pan and place on waxed paper. Knead, cool, and place in a closed container.

STUFF an old duffle bag or pillowcase with rags, foam rubber, etc., to make a punching bag. Hang it with heavy twine in a corner of the room. Punching the bag helps get rid of lots of tension and pent-up energy. (You may want to use it yourself from time to time!)

It's the little things we do and the minor words we say That make or break the beauty of the average passing day.

HELP your child build a positive attitude toward self and others by following these suggestions:

Nip negative behavior in the bud before it goes too far.

Give positive redirection.

Respond sensitively to the child as you observe him or her closely.

Be specific, not general, in praise or correction.

Plan a neat, clean environment to inspire good behavior.

Use praise and love-oriented discipline rather than force.

Let the child know you love him for himself, unconditionally.

FAMILY DEVOTIONS can do much to draw the family into a closer relationship with itself and with God. Here are some suggestions for effectively sharing God's Word within the family.

Involve children. They can read Bible stories, lead in prayer, select hymns to sing.

Memorize Bible verses together as a family.

Use a book of printed devotions for guidance. These are available from your local church or Christian bookstore.

Use a Bible when reading the Scripture verses, even if you are using a book of devotions.

Ask questions for discussion about the Scriptures you have read or about the printed devotion.

Share things which happened during the day that had spiritual significance.

Close the devotions with prayer. Each family member should have opportunity to offer prayers.

Teenage daughter (as the radio ground out the final notes of the latest hit song): "Did you ever hear anything so wonderful?" Father: "Only once when a truck loaded with empty milk cans bumped another truck filled with live ducks."

Be strong and take heart, all you who hope in the Lord. —Psalm 31:24

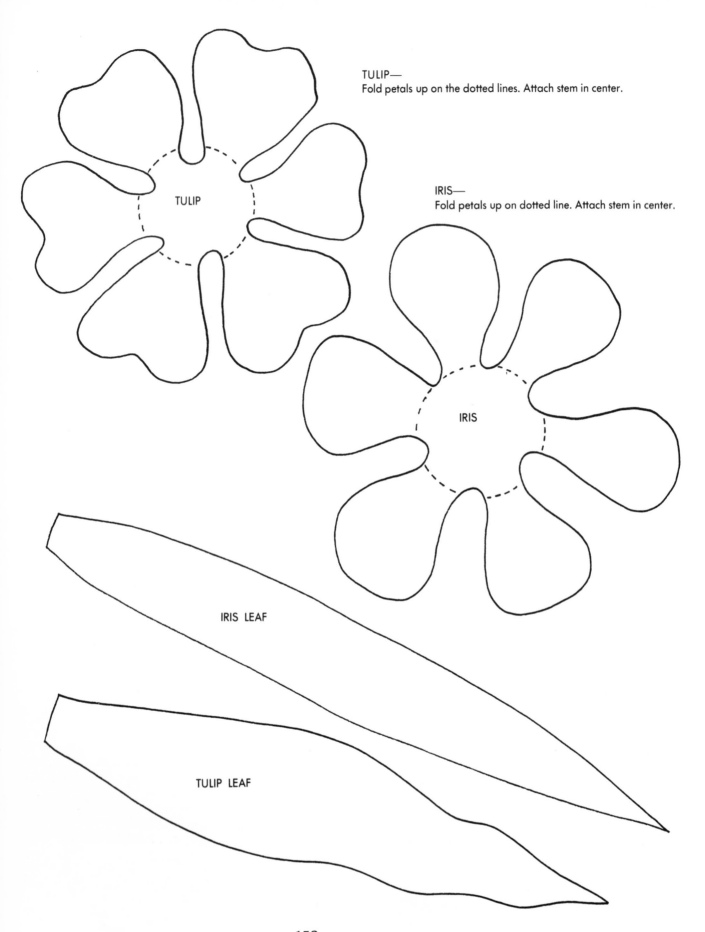

TULIP—
Fold petals up on the dotted lines. Attach stem in center.

IRIS—
Fold petals up on dotted line. Attach stem in center.

TULIP

IRIS

IRIS LEAF

TULIP LEAF

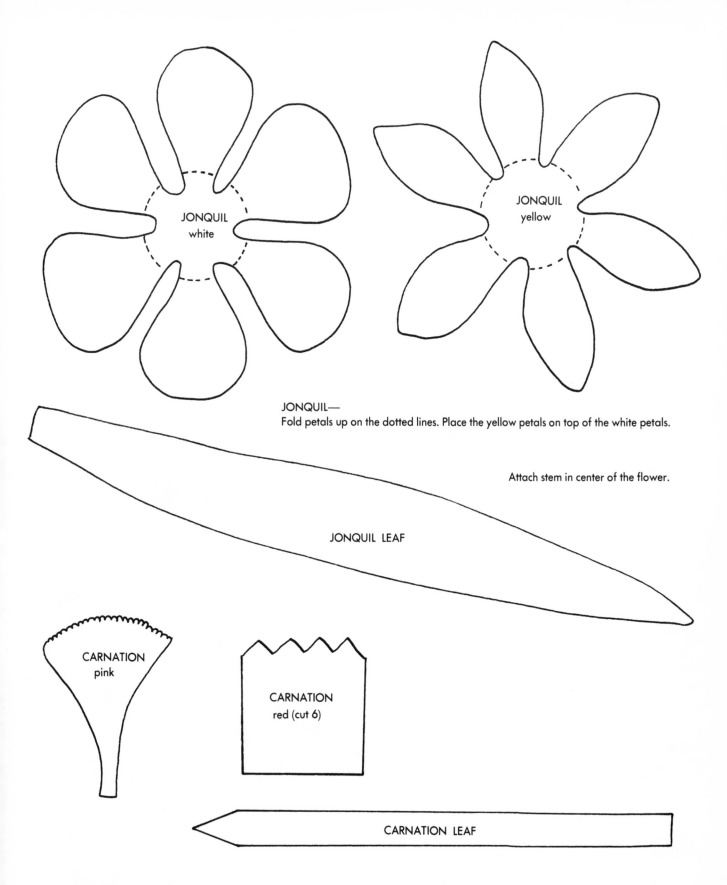

JONQUIL—
Fold petals up on the dotted lines. Place the yellow petals on top of the white petals.

Attach stem in center of the flower.

JONQUIL LEAF

CARNATION
pink

CARNATION
red (cut 6)

CARNATION LEAF

CARNATION—
Roll the pink center. Wrap the 6 red petals around the center and attach stem.

LEAF PATTERNS

OAK

MAPLE

ELM

COTTONWOOD

BIRCH

ASH

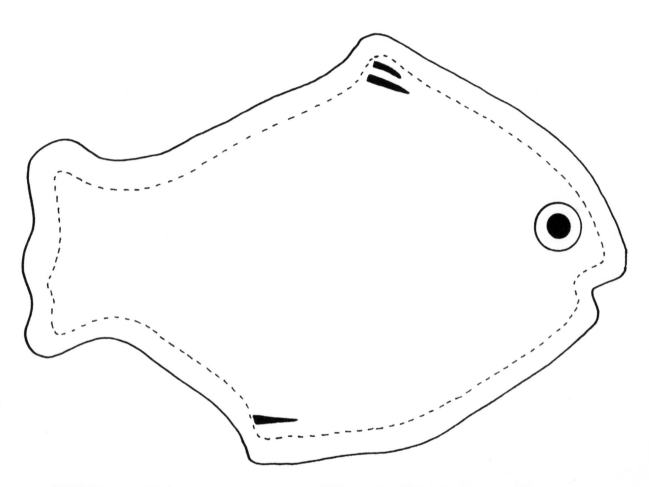

BEANBAG. Cut two fish from scraps of durable cloth—a bright color if possible. Embroider eyes and fins or glue pieces of felt for these features. Stitch the two pieces together on the wrong side. Allow a ¼-inch seam. Leave opening at tail. Turn right side out. Fill with navy beans—not too full. Sew opening together.

STAR

BUTTERFLY

HEART

BELL

156

CHRISTMAS ANGEL. Cut on the lines. Interlock slits A and B. Fold arms C and D forward. The angel can stand by itself or a string can be attached at dot E for hanging. Use foil or construction paper for the angels.

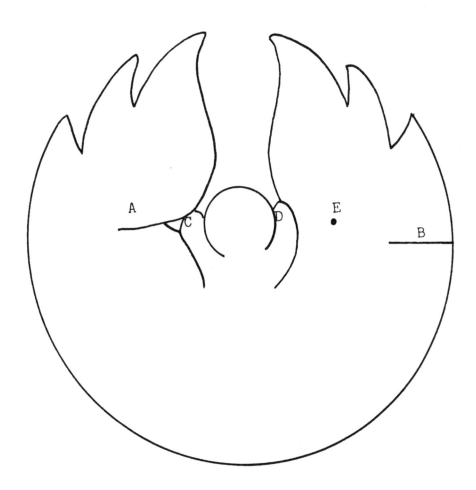

SUNDIAL
Put it in the sun to tell time.

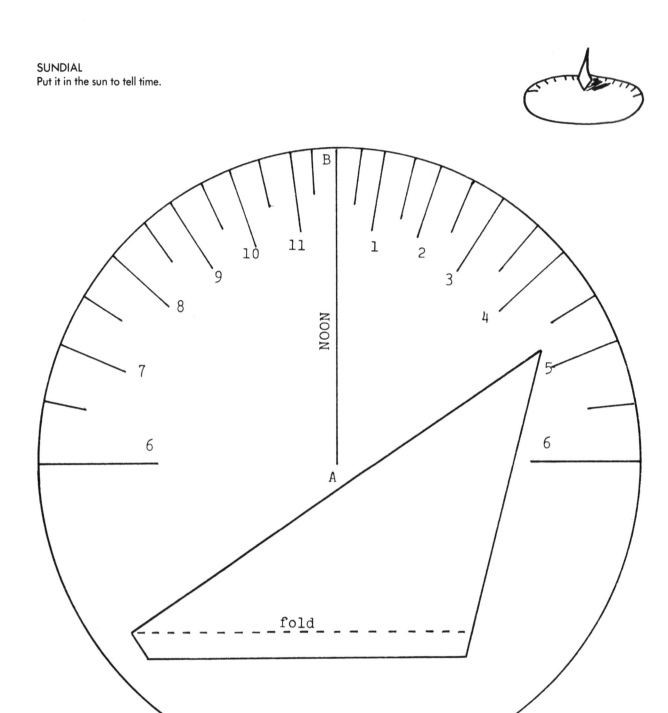

Trace the patterns onto a piece of heavy cardboard. Cut out circle, and then cut out separately the triangle. Make all the markings around the edge of the circle. Now attach triangular piece to circle by pasting folded tab in place as shown on the pattern.

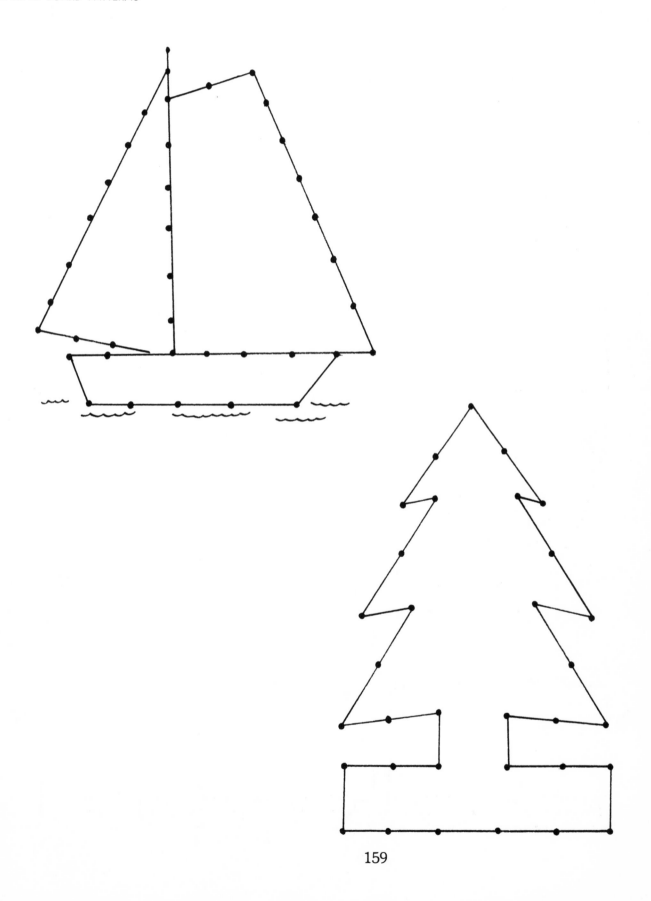

WOODEN BUILDING BLOCKS cut from a 4-foot board 4-inches square.

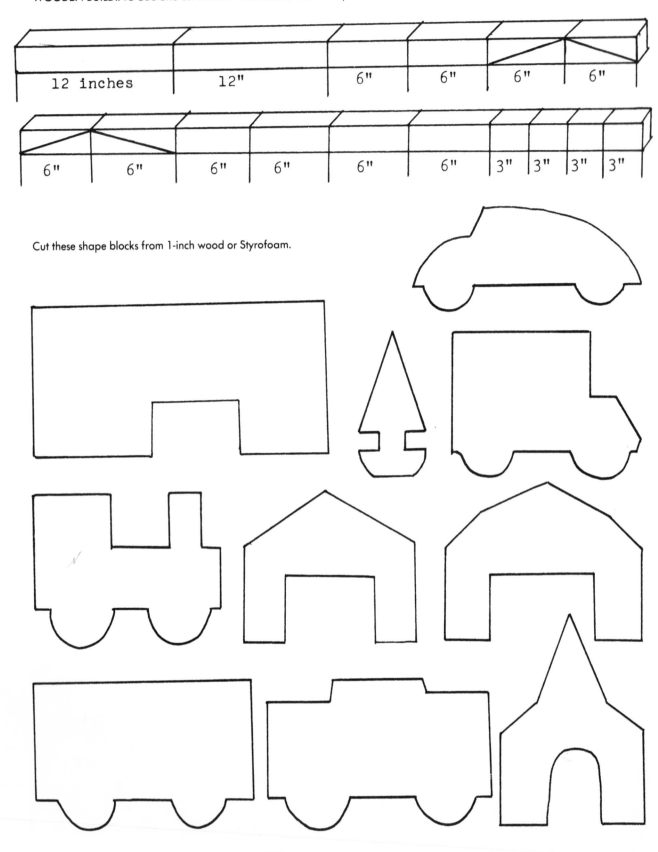

| 12 inches | 12" | 6" | 6" | 6" | 6" |

| 6" | 6" | 6" | 6" | 6" | 6" | 3" | 3" | 3" | 3" |

Cut these shape blocks from 1-inch wood or Styrofoam.

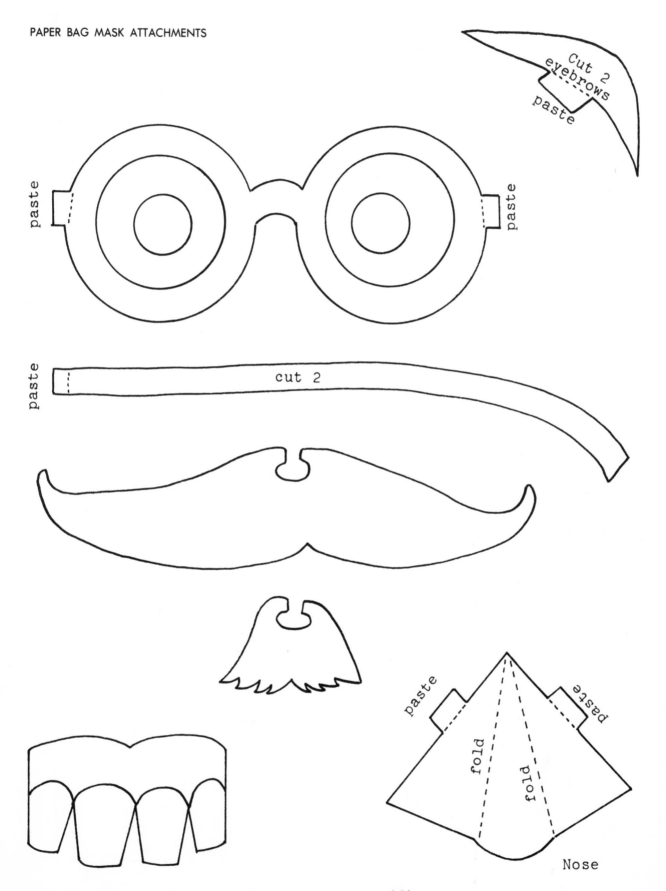

GEOMETRIC SHAPES
Cut on solid lines. Fold on dotted lines. Paste tabs to assemble.

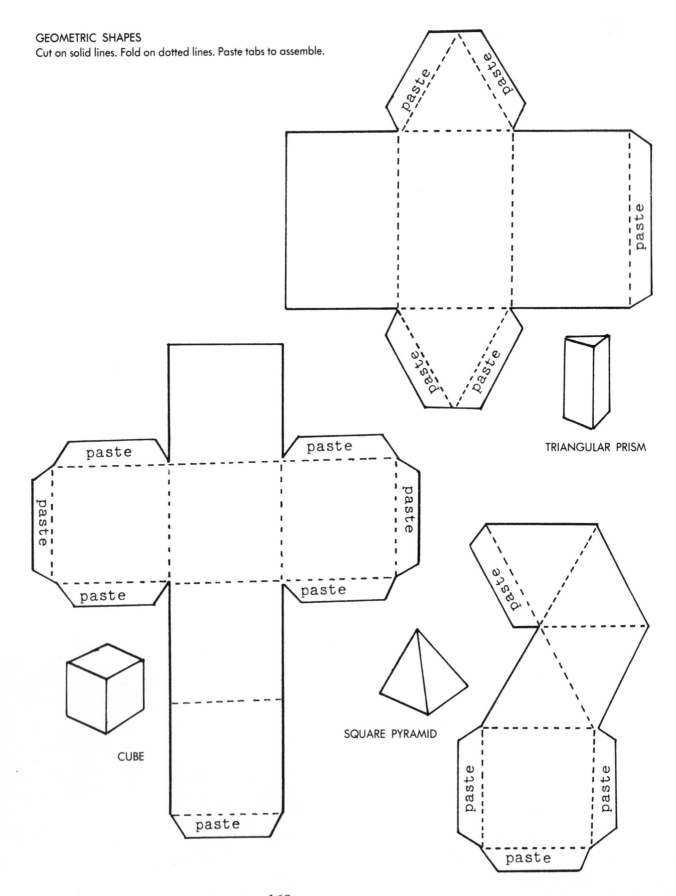

TRIANGULAR PRISM

CUBE

SQUARE PYRAMID

GEOMETRIC SHAPES
Cut on solid lines. Fold on dotted lines. Paste tabs to assemble.

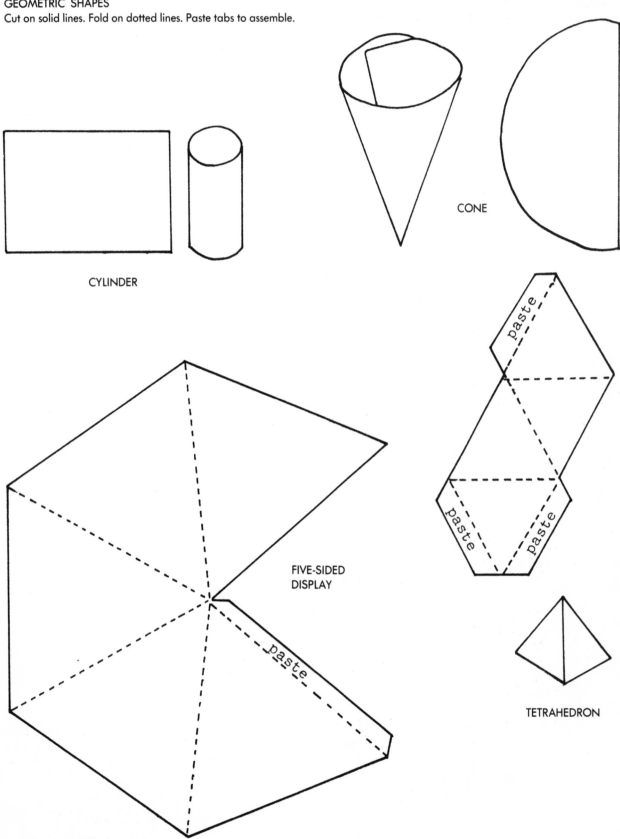

CONE

CYLINDER

paste

FIVE-SIDED
DISPLAY

paste

paste

paste

paste

TETRAHEDRON

THREE-DIMENSIONAL ALPHABET

Experiment with making a standing 3-D alphabet by cutting the following shapes from heavy paper or cardboard
Paste them together for the different letters.

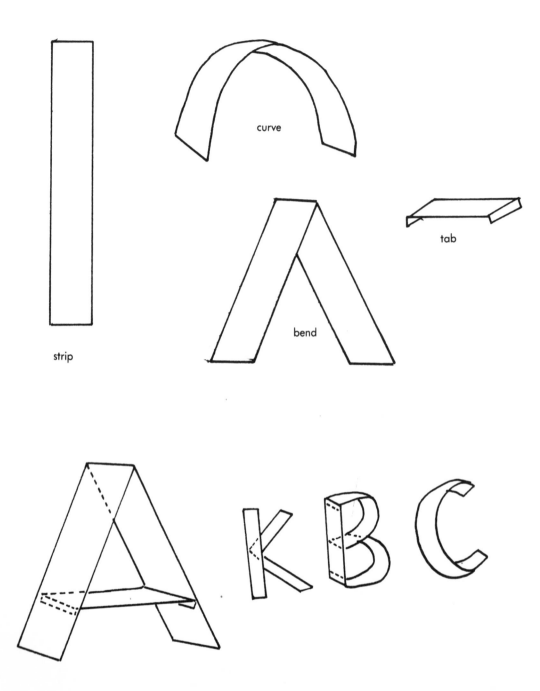

curve

tab

strip

bend

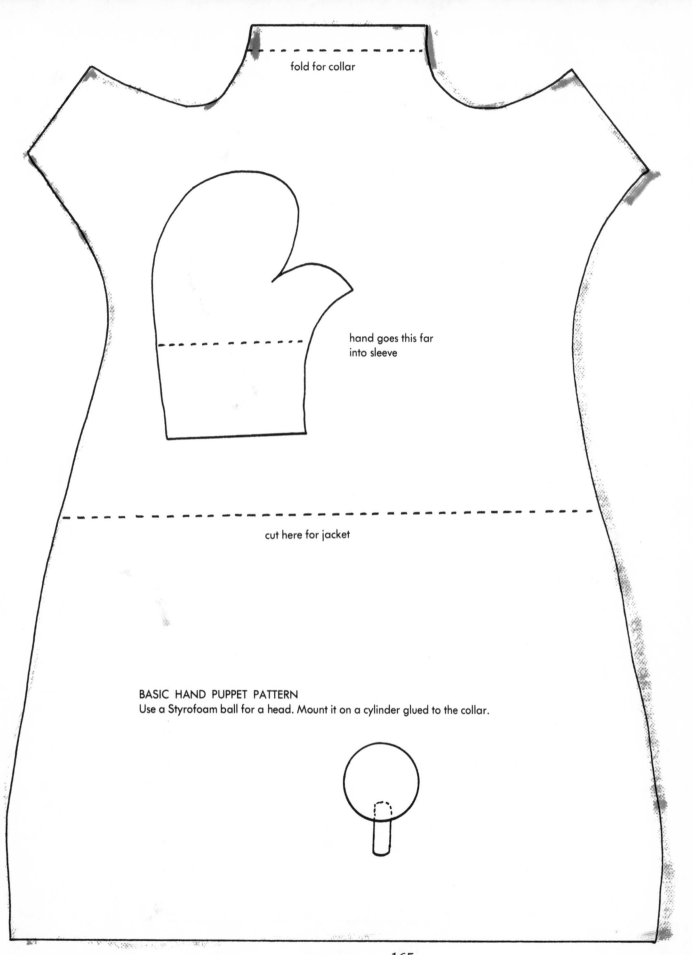

fold for collar

hand goes this far
into sleeve

cut here for jacket

BASIC HAND PUPPET PATTERN
Use a Styrofoam ball for a head. Mount it on a cylinder glued to the collar.

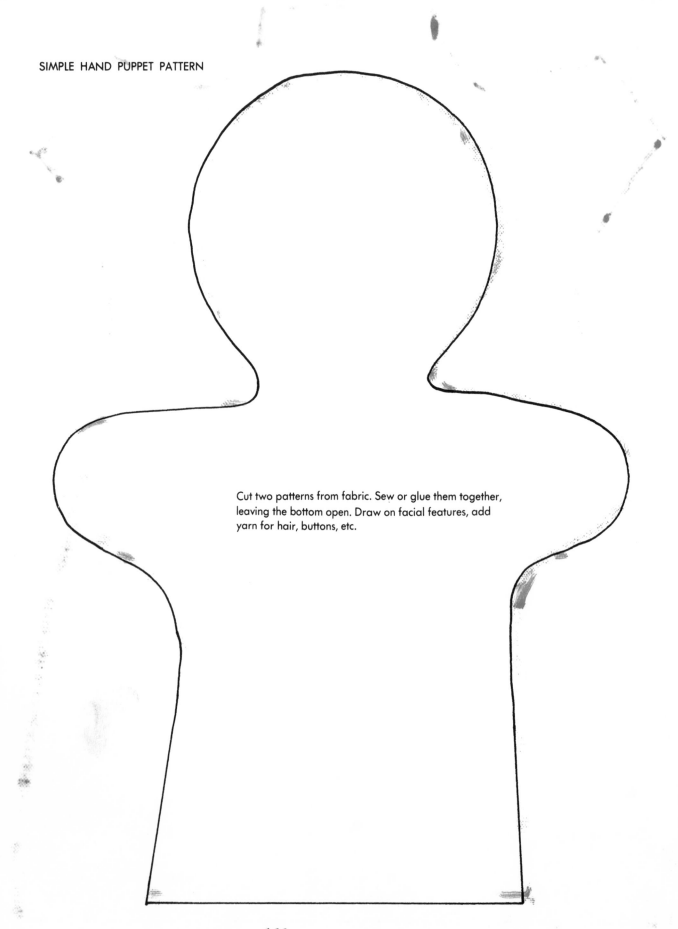

Cut two patterns from fabric. Sew or glue them together, leaving the bottom open. Draw on facial features, add yarn for hair, buttons, etc.

BASIC MARIONETTE DESIGN

Use wood blocks and dowels for the parts. Eye hooks for the joints. Dress the marionette and add a face, hair, etc. Move the marionette by moving the strings attached to flat control boards.

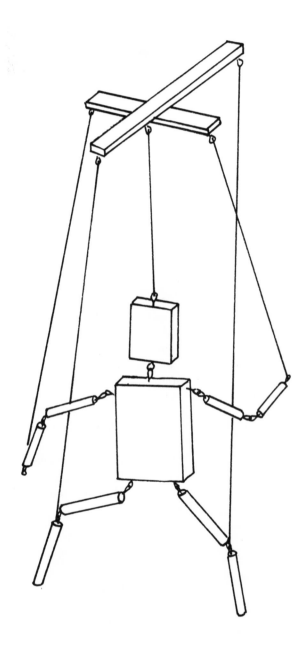

INDEX

THE AUTHOR

Nancy S. Williamson, a commissioned minister of Christian education, served the Federal Way, Washington, Church of the Nazarene and Galilean Chapel, Ocean Shores, Washington. She was owner and administrator of Children's World Christian School of Seattle, a day care, preschool, and kindergarten for eighty children ages two-and-one-half to eight.

Miss Williamson attended Puget Sound College of the Bible, Seattle Pacific University, and the Church of the Nazarene Study Program for ministers and ministers of Christian education.

Other published works include several teacher training articles and teaching aids for *Leader Guidebook, Success, Early Years, Day Care & Early Education, Instructor,* and *Evangelizing Today's Child* magazines; nursery, kindergarten, primary, and junior curriculum aids for David C. Cook Publishing Company; multimedia teaching kits on Bible customs and Bible geography; and daily devotions for *Christ in Our Home,* Augsburg Publishing House.

Miss Williamson's other books include *Handy Helpful Household Hints* (Bible Voice), *100 Handy Ideas for Busy Teachers* (Baker), and *If You Lived in Bible Times* (Scripture Press).